DYNAMITE NETWORKING
FOR DYNAMITE JOBS

Books and CD-ROMs by Drs. Ron and Caryl Krannich

The Almanac of International Jobs and Careers
Best Jobs For the 1990s and Into the 21st Century
Change Your Job, Change Your Life
The Complete Guide to International Jobs and Careers
The Complete Guide to Public Employment
The Directory of Federal Jobs and Employers
Discover the Best Jobs For You!
Dynamite Answers to Interview Questions
Dynamite Cover Letters
Dynamite Networking For Dynamite Jobs
Dynamite Resumes
Dynamite Salary Negotiations
Dynamite Tele-Search
The Educator's Guide to Alternative Jobs and Careers
Find a Federal Job Fast!
From Air Force Blue to Corporate Gray
From Army Green to Corporate Gray
From Navy Blue to Corporate Gray
High Impact Resumes and Letters
Interview For Success
Job Search Letters That Get Results
Job-Power Source CD-ROM
Jobs and Careers With Nonprofit Organizations
Jobs For People Who Love Computers and the Information Highway
Jobs For People Who Love Health Care and Nursing
Jobs For People Who Love Hotels, Resorts, and Cruise Ships
Jobs For People Who Love to Work From Home
Jobs For People Who Love Travel
Mayors and Managers
Moving Out of Education
Moving Out of Government
The Politics of Family Planning Policy
Re-Careering in Turbulent Times
Resumes and Cover Letters For Transitioning Military Personnel
Shopping and Traveling in Exotic Asia
Shopping in Exciting Australia and Papua New Guinea
Shopping in Exotic Places
Shopping the Exotic South Pacific
Treasures and Pleasures of Hong Kong
Treasures and Pleasures of India
Treasures and Pleasures of Indonesia
Treasures and Pleasures of Italy
Treasures and Pleasures of Morocco
Treasures and Pleasures of Paris and the French Riviera
Treasures and Pleasures of Singapore and Malaysia
Treasures and Pleasures of Thailand
Treasures and Pleasures of the Philippines
Ultimate Job Source CD-ROM

DYNAMITE NETWORKING FOR DYNAMITE JOBS

101 Interpersonal, Telephone, and Electronic Techniques For Getting Job Leads, Interviews and Offers

Ronald L. Krannich, Ph.D.
Caryl Rae Krannich, Ph.D.

IMPACT PUBLICATIONS
Manassas Park, VA

DYNAMITE NETWORKING FOR DYNAMITE JOBS

Library of Congress Cataloguing-in-Publication Data

Krannich, Ronald L.
    Dynamite networking for dynamite jobs: 101 interpersonal, telephone, and electronic techniques for getting job leads, interviews, and offers / Ronald L. Krannich, Caryl Rae Krannich.
      p. c.m
    Rev. ed. of The new network your way to job and career success.
    Includes bibliographical references and index.
    ISBN: 1-57023-059-5 (alk. paper)
    1. Job hunting. 2. Career development. 3. Social networks
I. Krannich, Caryl Rae. II. Title. III. Title: New network your way to job and career success.
HF5382.7.K7   1996
650.14--dc20   96-11620
                                                      CIP

For information on distribution or quantity discount rates, Tel. 703/361-7300, Fax 703/335-9486, e-mail impactp@erols.com, or write to: Sales Department, IMPACT PUBLICATIONS, 9104-N Manassas Drive, Manassas Park, VA 22111. Distributed to the trade by National Book Network, 4720 Boston Way, Suite A, Lanham, MD 20706, Tel. 301/459-8696.

CONTENTS

CHAPTER 3

Networks, Networking, and Your Job Search 36

CHAPTER 4

Myths, Abuses, and
Misuses of Networks 59

DYNAMITE NETWORKING FOR DYNAMITE JOBS

1

TODAY'S BEST KEPT SECRET TO JOB SUCCESS

Successful job seekers and career climbers do something different from others—they know how to network their way to job and career success. Rather than sit passively on the sidelines waiting for jobs to come to them, they develop proactive strategies for finding jobs and advancing their careers. They acquire employment information and leads by using the telephone, working professional meetings and social gatherings, writing and following up letters, and using online computer services. Collectively known as "networking," these activities lead to job interviews and offers. When used on the job, these same strategies can accelerate one's career advancement.

THE SECRET LANGUAGE OF SUCCESS

Networking, networking, networking!

There must be something magical in those words. For those who understand what networking is all about, this term equates with job and career success. It's the secret language of effective job seekers and career advancers. It's the key to unlocking the doors of prospective employers.

Be it in your personal or professional life, networking can achieve amazing results. It can be applied to many different situations and settings, depending on your goals. If, as we assume throughout this book, your goal is to find a job, networking will quickly put you in contact with employers and help you locate numerous unadvertised positions. If used properly, networking can become your ticket to job and career success. It can cut your job search time in half, put you into high quality jobs, and hasten your long-term career advancement. You will acquire the street smarts for easily changing jobs and advancing your career.

WHERE DO YOU GO, WHAT DO YOU DO?

Success in finding employment, keeping jobs, and advancing careers involves much more than acquiring impressive educational credentials, demonstrating powerful skills and abilities, mailing dynamite resumes and job search letters, making cold calls, using online electronic job search services, or implementing a well conceived plan of action.

Whatever your qualifications, good intentions, or electronic prowess, you must clearly communicate your qualifications to employers in the most efficient and effective manners possible. **You** must let potential employers know that **you** are the one who will most likely add the greatest value to their operations.

But how can you best communicate your qualifications to potential employers, especially given the highly competitive nature of today's job market? Let's face reality. You're competing with hundreds—perhaps thousands—of individuals who have mastered the art of responding to classified job ads with well-crafted resumes and letters. Some use aggressive telephone tactics or get an inside track to employers through connections with influential people. Many even hire employment specialists to help them find a job.

Where do you go and what do you plan to do next? How are you going to chart your path to job and career success?

The central purpose of a job search is very simple—communicate your qualifications to employers.

COMMUNICATE YOUR QUALIFICATIONS TO EMPLOYERS

Despite all that is written and prescribed about finding jobs and changing careers, the central purpose of a job search is very simple—communicate your qualifications to potential employers. Since most of these employers will be strangers, you must use an approach that enables you to effectively introduce yourself to strangers as well as convince strangers to offer you a job. Needless to say, this is not your normal way of doing business with others—especially with strangers!

If you focus laser-like on this single purpose, you will be surprised how successful you will become in your job search. You'll stop wasting time on activities that contribute little or nothing to this central purpose. Again, you want to communicate your qualifications to potential employers whom you must sufficiently motivate to offer you a job.

Networking is the most important process by which you can communicate your qualifications to employers. While networking in general can enrich your social and professional life, when applied to the job search, networking becomes the key dynamic for opening the doors of employers who ordinarily would not know about you nor seriously consider you for a job. It is this process—networking—that you can and must learn and put into practice if you are to become most effective in your job search as well as on the job.

GET AMAZING RESULTS

That's our task in the following pages—to show you how networking skills play a central role in conducting an effective job search. Page after page provide you with practical advice on how to develop your own networking skills which you can immediately put into practice with amazing results.

If you follow our guidance, you should more than double your job search effectiveness. You will learn to communicate your qualifications loud and clear to hundreds of potential employers you would have failed to contact had you not discovered this book. Better still, once you get the job, you will continue to use your networking skills to ensure your future job and career success.

While your job future may appear uncertain, with sound networking skills you need never be without a job.

While your job future may appear uncertain, with sound networking skills you need never be without a job. Chances are you will find jobs and advance in careers that are a "fit" for your particular mix of motivated interests, skills, and abilities.

QUESTION SUCCESS

Why are some people more successful at finding jobs and advancing careers than others? Are they more intelligent, skilled, and motivated than the average person? Perhaps they are luckier or they have the right connections to people who have the power to hire.

Or perhaps they do something different from others when looking for employment or advancing on the job.

Maybe they are well organized and have a clear idea of what they want to do. They probably write excellent resumes and letters, target key individuals and organizations, and perform well in job interviews. Could they also be excellent networkers?

How can you best find a job and advance your career in today's job market? Is it proper to influence the hiring process by using "connections" to by-pass formal hiring procedures? When and how should one use others in gaining access to employers as well as getting ahead on the job?

What is this thing called "networking" that everyone talks about when looking for jobs? Is it something I need to learn and use in my own job search?

These questions frequently confront individuals who are conducting a job search or attempting to advance their career within an organization. They are central concerns in the pages that follow. For these questions need to be addressed in practical how-to terms so you will have a better understanding of how to identify, build, and use your own networks for finding jobs and advancing your career in the years ahead.

CONFUSED, ABUSED, AND MISUSED

Few terms are so confused, abused, and misused as "networks" and "networking." The confusion, misuse, and abuse take place on both the conceptual and practical levels. It's a WYKWIM—*"Well, You Know What I Mean"*—concept. Indeed, the concepts are seldom clearly defined. Job seekers and career advancers, for example, are told they should use their "networks" to get ahead, and the key to job search success is "networking." Therefore, some of the so-called facts of job search life are that *"You have to network"* and *"Networking is the key to uncovering job leads, getting job interviews, and being promoted on the job."* The terms are used so freely that one assumes everyone should know what this is all about and that many are doing it with considerable success!

On a more practical level, job seekers are often told that networking involves *"contacting the people who have the power to hire,"* as if busy hiring officials have nothing better to do than to be pestered by job seekers who ostensibly only want "information and advice" rather than a "job interview and offer." Or they are told to join professional associations that will provide them with networking opportunities—as if other members of the organization have nothing better to do than to be bothered by "networkers" who have little interest in an organization other than using it to exchange business cards and collect names, addresses, and telephone numbers for developing job leads which, in turn, leads to pestering even more people in one's new-found network. Indeed, we know people, including ourselves, who have dropped their membership in professional associations precisely because they have become popular centers for "networkers" who abuse the organization for their own employment gains. They become dens of name-droppers and business card exchangers who want nothing more than to collect more names and referrals for building and using their own networks.

The basic problem with networks and networking lies with those who recommend the building and use of networks and networking. On the one hand, writers tell you networks and networking are important, but they never define these terms in practical how-to terms. At best they outline "principles" of networking, present vague examples of what networking involves, or include anecdotal cases of successful networking.

On the other hand, many writers give practical guidance that often leads to the very abuses that give networking such a bad name—contact those who have the power to hire and join professional associations. They legitimize an assertive job seeker who attempts to acquire influence in the hiring process. As a result, many career counselors are reluctant to recommend networking strategies or they rightfully criticize it as being overstated and overrated in importance as well as frequently abusive in application.

TOWARD A MORE ETHICAL
AND PRACTICAL APPROACH

We believe networking is the key process for conducting a successful job search as well as for keeping jobs and advancing careers. However, networks and networking need to be better defined and specified in both ethical and practical how-to terms then heretofore attempted. The confusion, abuses, and misuses of networks and networking must be avoided if you are to develop and use networks to their maximum advantage. Our approach does not require you to become an extroverted, aggressive salesperson who uncovers new job leads through cold-calling methods. Nor do you need to deceive others or abuse organizations by playing an "information and advice" game when you are actually attempting to use people to get "job interviews and offers."

Our approach to networks and networking begins with a basic ethical emphasis: You must be completely honest with both yourself and others when seeking employment or advancing your career. While you can learn to play new roles for new situations, such role playing involves acting out scripts that are unfamiliar to most people. These role players eventually will be discovered for what they really are—individuals who may behave very differently from the role they learned to temporarily play in order to get a job interview and offer. Once they get the job and begin displaying their normal patterns of behavior—that have little relationship to the roles they played in getting the job—they may experience on-the-job difficulties that will require something more than an additional round of newly acquired role playing behaviors. Indeed, their employer may discover that he or she has once again been deceived by a job applicant who learned all the "ins" and "outs" of getting a job interview and offer. They were good networkers who knew how to get the job interview and offer but they were poor job performers.

You must be completely honest with both yourself and others when seeking employment or advancing your career.

Our approach to networks and networking is also practical. We go beyond examples of successful networking and listings of networking sources to provide you with the basic building blocks for identifying, developing, and using your own networks in the process of finding employment and advancing your career. Our concepts are defined so they can be translated into practical use. In so doing, we include models and examples designed to build key networking skills. Once you translate these concepts into practical use by following the models and examples, you should be able to make networking a permanent part of your job and career behavior. Above all, you need not develop a new personality nor become an aggressive and manipulative individual intent on making others do things your way.

GO BEYOND ROLE PLAYING

Most job search advice is based on a very simple principle that makes the job search both easy and difficult for most people: learn to play different roles for different situations. For some people, role playing is easy; they learn the expectations of others, copy examples, and change their behavior accordingly. Consequently, if employers want to see candidates who are energetic, competent, and likable, then you should dish out energy, competence, and likability on resumes and in interviews by the way you write (use action verbs and focus on achievements), talk (use positives and be enthusiastic), and appear in person (dress for success).

While this role approach makes sense because it is designed to meet employer's expectations—and at times exceed them—this approach is very difficult for many individuals to follow because it requires role playing which does not come naturally to them. Outside the make-believe world of the theater and movies, playing a role in real life—specially when looking for a job—verges on being dishonest with others: you must temporarily behave like someone you are not in order to get and pass the job interview. To be told to acquire a temporary set of new behaviors—to take on stage before strangers who have the power to hire—is beyond both the motivation and capacity of most individuals. Making cold calls to uncover job leads or contacting people with the power to hire may make sense in a job search, but these activities are best done by people who are naturally assertive, aggressive, and perhaps obnoxious in their relations with strangers. They simply don't come naturally to most people who are choosy about how and with whom they will associate.

Such role playing also borders on being unethical sales tactics. Emphasizing form over substance, such role playing does not reveal the individual's real qualifications nor project future performance in mean-ingful ways. Worst of all, this approach results in canned and meaning-less resume language (*"Enjoy working with people"*) and stock answers to interview questions (*"My education helped prepare me..."*) that raise troubling questions about what information is actually being exchanged in the job search and hiring processes. Are you communicating your qualifications or manipulating forms in lieu of content? Not surprising, role playing often confuses form with content.

For employers, this process at times becomes a disappointing role playing ritual of sorts. After interviewing the 100th candidate dressed in a similar blue suit, carrying a leather briefcase, communicating positive nonverbal behaviors (firm handshake and good eye contact), and answer-ing all the questions according to the textbook, employers begin won-dering about the efficacy of engaging themselves and candidates in the traditional recruitment and evaluation processes. These processes may have for all intents and purposes been negated by well prepared can-didates who know how to play the proper roles of "good applicant" and "good interviewee." They are well-versed in key job search "strategies and techniques" that are supposed to really work for getting a job. No wonder interviewers increasingly opt for conducting behavior-based interviews that cut through most of the traditional interview role playing as they attempt to get at the real performance capabilities of candidates.

Contrary to what many job search strategies and techniques may suggest, employers are not stupid. They still look for content, substance, and value—the key elements that define the value of jobs. They want to accurately predict performance rather than risk hiring a potential problem employee.

A more ethical and realistic approach to the job search and career advancement is one that focuses on building new skills rather than a new set of role behaviors. Therefore, we are concerned with the process of building and using networks as a permanent aspect of one's career rather than something you only do when you need to find a job or advance your career. The skill becomes part of your daily patterns of behavior. As such, it becomes natural and reveals the real you.

Contrary to what many job search strategies and techniques may suggest, employers are not stupid. They still look for content, substance, and value.

CHANGE YOUR BEHAVIOR

Each of us has learned behaviors, habits, or patterns we reinforce daily. Many of these behaviors generate positive responses from others; but some of them are bad habits we should break. For example, how well do you communicate over the telephone, physically appear to others, or ask and answer questions? Do you stutter, fidget, or lose eye contact when nervous? Do you talk too much or too little? Are you too shy to contact strangers? Do you have a habit of being late for appointments? These are all examples of behaviors we can change if we are strongly **motivated** to do so. But it is easy to slip back into the old patterns if we are not careful.

If you feel you need to break certain habits and learn new behaviors, you can make long-term changes without resorting to temporary role playing. You must first be aware of the undesirable behavior you wish to replace as well as the desirable behavior you wish to acquire. Second, you must be aware of the undesirable behavior whenever it takes place. For this you may need to enlist the aid of your spouse or good friend; ask them to: *"Please observe me and inform me whenever I am doing ____ _____."* After a while you will develop greater awareness of the particular behavior.

Once we are conscious of our behavior, gradually we will become alert to our behavior early enough to alter it. Given even more time of diligent awareness, the new behavior replaces the old one and eventually becomes as natural as the undesirable behavior once was. By incorporating the new behavior into your ongoing patterns of behavior, you will learn to go beyond role playing that plagues much of the well-meaning advice on how to conduct an effective job search.

Developing an effective networking campaign that leads to getting a job that is right for you should be sufficient reason to motivate you to change some of your behaviors. If you think a behavior may be holding you back, try changing it now. The more time you give yourself, the more likely the change will become permanent and the less likely you will slip back into your former behavior.

USE USEFUL RESOURCES

Each year millions of job hunters turn to career planning books for assistance. Normally they begin with a general book and next turn to resume and interview books.

The reasons for choosing this sequence of books is simple. Job hunters should begin with a sound understanding of all elements contributing to a successful job search and then focus on specific job search activities, or what we call job search steps, which have the greatest payoffs: resume and letter writing, networking, and interviewing. Until the first edition of this book appeared in 1989, a practical networking book had not been available as the critical bridge between a resume and an interview book.

While we are primarily concerned at this stage in taking you through the networking stage of a job search, we also recognize the need to continue through other important stages that result in meeting potential employers and receiving job offers. These other steps are outlined in our other books: *Change Your Job Change Your Life, Discover the Best Jobs For You, High Impact Resumes and Letters, Dynamite Resumes, Dynamite Cover Letters, Job Search Letters That Get Results, Dynamite Answers to Interview Questions, Interview For Success, Dynamite Tele-Search,* and *Dynamite Salary Negotiations.* We also address particular job and career fields in the following books: *The Best Jobs For the 1990s and Into the 21st Century, The Complete Guide to Public Employment, Find a Federal Job Fast!, The Complete Guide to International Jobs and Careers, The Directory of Federal Jobs and Employers, The Almanac of International Jobs and Careers, Jobs For People Who Love Travel,* and *The Educator's Guide to Alternative Jobs and Careers.* These and many other job search books are outlined in Chapter 9. They are available in many bookstores and libraries. For your convenience, they also can be ordered directly from Impact Publications by completing the order form at the end of this book.

Impact Publications also publishes a catalog of additional job and career resources. To receive a free copy of this listing, send a self-addressed stamped envelope (#10 business size) to:

IMPACT PUBLICATIONS
ATTN: Career Resource List
9104-N Manassas Drive
Manassas Park, VA 22111-5211

You also may want to visit their World Wide Web site for a complete listing of career resources: http://www.impactpublications.com. Their site contains some of the most important career and job finding resources available today, including many titles that are difficult, if not impossible, to find in bookstores and libraries. You will find everything from additional networking books to books on self-assessment, resume and letter writing, interviewing, government and international jobs, military, women, minorities, entrepreneurs as well as CD-ROM programs, software, and videos. This is an excellent resource for keeping in touch with the major resources that can assist you with every stage of your job search and with your future career development plans.

COMING UP

This is not a book primarily about where the networks are and how you can use them to get a job or advance your career. Nor is this a book about networking in general nor electronic networking via the Internet. As we will see later, there are numerous resources for identifying organizations that function as networks. These organizations can play an important role in finding, keeping, and advancing jobs and careers. Other books examine useful networking techniques such as small talk and mingling in groups for business and social purposes. And still other focus solely on electronic networking or interpersonal networking. This book, instead, focuses on networks and networking for the purpose of finding jobs and advancing careers both interpersonally and electronically. It shows you how to identify, expand, engage, use, develop, and maintain networks appropriate to your own job and career goals. As such, this is the first book to focus on **developing both interpersonal and electronic networking skills** that can be used in many different settings and situations. We also include in Chapter 8, *"Organizations As Networking Resources,"* a useful listing of professional organizations that function as networking sources for individuals with different professional interests and goals.

The chapters that follow are designed to be "user-friendly." They proceed from a definition of key concepts to explanations of how to identify, develop, and use networks as part of your permanent skill pattern for finding jobs and advancing your career. Chapter 2, *"Finding Jobs and Advancing Careers in the Decade Ahead,"* provides the employment setting for examining networks and networking in the job markets of today and tomorrow. Placed within the context of 29 major changes taking place within the job market over the coming decade, this chapter discusses how important networking will become in the future.

Chapter 3, *"Networks, Networking, and Your Job Search,"* outlines the major concepts central to the remaining chapters. Here we define the concepts of networks and networking and show how they relate to job search techniques, processes, and goals. The chapter assists you in identifying your own network as well as illustrates how your network can be linked to the networks of others. In this chapter we also identify seven steps in the job search process that are central to understanding the key role networking plays in the job search. The chapter concludes with a discussion of how networking relates to your overall job search campaign.

Chapter 4, *"Myths, Abuses, and Misuses of Networks,"* examines 19 key myths and several additional realities surrounding the use and abuse of networks and networking. These myths and realities are responsible for many networking and job search failures. Moreover, they discourage many individuals from developing what we see as positive networking skills that are both ethical and practical. By outlining the realities of these myths, we attempt to put to rest the objections to networking by those who criticize it for all the wrong reasons—its misuses and abuses—and clarify many of the issues surrounding networks and networking in the job search.

Chapter 5, *"Identifying and Building Your Networks,"* begins looking at the practical steps in the networking process by first examining your present network of relationships and then suggesting techniques—prospecting and networking—for expanding your networks. It concludes with a discussion of how to handle one of the most important problems encountered in the process of building networks—potential rejections.

Chapter 6, *"Developing Job Leads and Getting Job Interviews,"* takes you face-to-face with network contacts and potential employers by examining the major use of networks in the job search process—the informational interview. Beginning with the perspective of employers, we then turn to the job seeker in focusing on the details of approaching people by telephone and letter as well as meeting them in person for the purpose of acquiring information, advice, and referrals. This chapter includes examples of effective letters and conversations. By way of summary it outlines key rules for networking success.

Chapter 7, *"Maintaining and Expanding Your Network,"* stresses the importance of networking as an on-going process for advancing one's career within an organization or profession. Stressing that networking is more than just another job finding technique, to be most effective, it must include follow-up, feedback, and routine networking activities within and between organizations.

Chapter 8, *"Organizations As Networking Resources,"* switches from the interpersonal process of networking to examples of formal professional organizations that function as important sources for building and maintaining your networks and networking activities. These organizations serve as starting points from which you can continue developing your own long-term networking skills.

Chapter 9, *"New Electronic Networking,"* reviews the operation of several electronic job search services that constitute new arenas for job networking. This chapter also identifies the major services by name, address, and phone number.

Chapter 10, *"Resources For Successful Job Networking,"* reviews some of the most important books and computer software on finding jobs and changing careers. This chapter is your guide to the best of the resources available on jobs and careers.

THE MORE YOU EXPLORE

Networking is not something you can turn on and off. As both a skill and an on-going process, networking is something individuals can and do learn. Some people are excellent networkers who acquired the skill as part of their early childhood development. They easily make friends and acquaintances and surround themselves with many individuals who can assist them in different ways. Making the right moves, they easily advance their careers by going to the right schools, joining the right organizations, and knowing the right people who like and trust them. They are simply good at developing, using, and nurturing personal relationships to their benefit.

However, most people are less extroverted and concerned with developing and maintaining personal relationships than the example of the successful networker. They must work at identifying their network and learning how to build, expand, and use it for job and career success. If pointed in the right direction with a few basic networking skills, these individuals also can achieve greater job and career success.

This is what this book is intended to do: provide you with basic networking skills so that you can further build and expand your networks in the coming years. It's a skill you can learn and use to ensure future job and career success. If you are like many other individuals who have learned our principles and put them into practice, you'll achieve amazing results as you put these networking skills to use.

The pages that follow explore the networking process for the purpose of building and expanding networking skills for all types of individuals who are concerned about achieving greater job and career success. If you follow our advice and put a few of our tips into practice, you should indeed achieve amazing results as you network your way to job and career success. You'll quickly develop dynamite networking skills that lead to dynamite jobs!

2

FINDING JOBS AND ADVANCING CAREERS IN THE DECADE AHEAD

Finding jobs and advancing careers in the decade ahead will require greater attention to the process of networking. For as competition for good jobs becomes keener and advancement opportunities become fewer, more and more individuals must learn to develop and use networks if they are to best achieve their goals and fulfill their career potential. Networking will take two major yet interdependent forms: interpersonal and electronic. Job seekers must learn how to develop and manage both types of networks.

JOB FINDING METHODS AND NETWORKING

Networking is nothing new or unusual. Indeed, the interpersonal nature of the job search is well documented. Since the 1930s studies of blue-collar, white-collar, managerial, technical, and professional workers have found that no more than 20 percent of placements occur through formal mechanisms. From 60 to 90 percent of jobs are found informally—mainly through friends, relatives, and direct contacts. The U.S. Department of Labor reports that 63.4 percent of all workers use informal job finding methods. Even with the highly structured government recruiting procedures, informal mechanisms play an important role in acquiring government employment.

Studies consistently show that formal and impersonal communications are the least effective means of getting a job. These include advertisements, public and private employment agencies, job listings provided by organizations, resume databases, and online job services. The most widely used and effective job finding methods are informal and personal: personal contacts and direct application. The personal contact is the major job-finding method, used by over 60 percent of all job seekers.

The most widely used and effective job finding methods are informal and personal: personal contacts and direct application.

Studies also note that both employers and employees **prefer** the informal and personal methods. Both groups believe personal contacts allow more in-depth, accurate, and up-to-date **information** which both groups need. Employers feel these methods **reduce recruiting costs and hiring risks**. Individuals who use personal contacts are more **satisfied** with their jobs; those who find jobs using formal methods tend to have a greater degree of job dissatisfaction. Those using informal methods tend to have **higher incomes**, and their jobs are in the highest income brackets.

It therefore comes as no surprise that networking is a widely used and effective job search technique. The basic question is this: How effective will **you** be in developing and using this technique in **your** job search?

CHANGES FOR THE COMING DECADE

We see several coming changes for jobs and careers in the decade ahead that will affect both the work force and the workplace. These changes also have major implications for networking. Stimulated by larger demographic and technological changes taking place in our global society, major changes are already emerging in the areas of job creation, youth, elderly, minorities, women, immigrants, part-time employment, service jobs, education and training, unions and labor-management relations, urban-rural shifts, regionalism, small businesses and entre-preneurship, and advancement opportunities.

The coming changes have important implications for job seekers and the methods they use in finding jobs and advancing careers. Taken together, these changes point to both dangers and new opportunities in the world of work. Moreover, they emphasize the important role networking should play in the job search process during the coming decade. They also emphasize the important role new electronic network-ing methods will play in bringing greater organization and centralization into an inherently decentralized and chaotic job market.

While many of these changes will create crises for millions of individuals who are not prepared to function in a rapidly changing job market, the same changes present new challenges and exciting opportuni-ties for those who understand how these changes will affect their own job and career future. Knowing what changes are likely to take place and preparing for these changes with the necessary knowledge, skills, and career development strategies will best enable you to turn seeming turbulence into new and hopefully exciting opportunities in the world of work.

LABOR FORCE AND INDUSTRY

CHANGE 1: **Shortage of competent workers, demonstrating basic literacy and learning skills, creates serious problems in developing an economy with an ade-quate work force for the jobs of the 21st century.**

Given the double-whammy of over 20 million functionally illiterate adults—or one-sixth of the potential labor force unable to read, write, or perform simple computations—and the availability of fewer easily trainable young entry-level workers, a large portion of the work force is destined to remain at the lowest end of the job market despite the fact that over 25 million new jobs will be created in the decade ahead. Most of these adults will remain permanently unemployed or underemployed while major labor shortages exist. As skill requirements rise rapidly for both entering and advancing within the work force, the nation's economic development will slow due to the lack of skilled workers. Both public and private sector worker literacy, basic education, and training programs will continue to expand, but their contribution to improving the overall skill levels of the work force will be minimal. The American economy and work force show classic signs of Second and Third World economies—potential economic performance out-strips the availability of a skilled work force.

CHANGE 2: **A strong and resurgent U.S. manufacturing sector, requiring increased automation and high-tech skills, creates few new jobs. Service industries will be responsible for most job growth in the coming decade. Most industries, including government, continue to downsize their operations and personnel in the quest for greater productivity and profit.**

Despite popular notions of the "decline" of American manufacturing industries, throughout the 1990s many of these industries followed the classic transformational model of American agriculture—increased productivity accompanied by the increased displacement of workers. During the past five years American manufacturing industry has become one of the strongest economic sectors in terms of production output but the weakest sector in terms of job growth and job creation. At the same time, American manufacturing has moved in the direction of what Peter Drucker calls a "production sharing system" by exporting the remaining high-cost, labor intensive aspects of the industries. As large manufacturing companies rebounded in the 1990s by becoming productive with smaller and more highly skilled work forces, many new manufacturing jobs developed among small manufacturing "job shops" employing fewer than 50 workers. The service industries, especially those in finance, retail, food, and healthcare, will continue to expand their work forces during the coming decade. "Productivity" and "management improvement" movements, frequently referred to as "downsizing," will continue among service industries as employers push for greater productivity because of (1) major labor shortages, and (2) the adaptation of new technology to increasingly inefficient, high-cost, labor intensive service industries, especially in the retail and healthcare industries. Government bureaucracies continue to "reinvent" themselves in the process of downsizing their operations and personnel. The result is keener competition for fewer job opportunities which require increased education and skills.

CHANGE 3:   **Unemployment remains naggingly high, fluctuating between a low of 5 percent and a high of 9 percent. It remains relatively predictable and permanent for certain segments of society.**

These fluctuations are attributed to a combination of boom and bust cycles in the economy as well as the persistence of structural unemployment exacerbated by millions of functionally illiterate adults on the periphery of the economy. Despite much publicized work-to-welfare reform and re-training efforts, finding steady and rewarding work becomes elusive for millions of individuals who remain ill-prepared for the new job market of the 21st century.

GOVERNMENT INITIATIVES AND CRISES

CHANGE 4:   **Government efforts to stimulate employment growth continues to be concentrated at the periphery of the job market.**

Most government programs aimed at generating jobs and resolving unemployment problems will be aimed at the poor and unskilled. These groups also are the least likely to relocate, use job search skills, develop standard work habits, or be trained in skills for tomorrow's job market. Given the mixed results from such programs and political pressures to experiment with some form of government-sponsored workfare programs, the government finally develops programs to directly employ the poor and unskilled on government programs as well as contract-out this class of unemployed to government contractors who will provide them with education and training along with work experience.

CHANGE 5:   **After difficult economic times during the first half of the 1990s, the U.S. deficit escalation finally subsides in the latter half of the 1990s and trade becomes more balanced as the U.S. slowly regains a more competitive international trade and debt position due to improved productivity of U.S. manufacturing industries and the devaluation of the U.S. dollar.**

International and domestic issues become closely tied to employment issues with increased exports to the booming economies of Asia and the Pacific Rim fueling job growth in the U.S. The government places increased emphasis on issues of unemployment, productivity, population growth, consumption, government bureaucratic and entitlement reform, and regional conflicts in Eastern Europe, the newly independent states of the former Soviet Union, the Middle East, and other Third and Fourth World countries that threaten the stability of international markets and thus long-term economic and employment growth in the U.S. Labor shortages become evident in the slow growth economy of the coming decade.

CHANGE 6: **A series of domestic and international crises— shocks and "unique events," some that already occurred in the 1980s and 1990s—emerge in the coming decade to create new boom and bust cycles contributing to high rates of unemployment.**

The most likely sources for the international crises will be problems developing among former communist regimes and poor Third and Fourth World nations: the disintegration of the nation-states in the former Soviet Union and a few former communist regimes in Eastern Europe; energy and precious metals shortages due to a depletion of current stocks and regional military conflicts; the collapse of financial markets due to default on international debts; and dislocation of lucrative resource and consumption markets due to continued wars in the Middle East, Africa, and South Asia. The most likely domestic crises center on financial markets, real estate, energy, water, and the environment. Crises in the banking and real estate markets continue to create major debt, credit, and bankruptcy problems for the economy. An energy crisis once again revitalizes the economies of Texas, Colorado, and Alaska. A new crisis—water shortages—in the rapidly developing Southwest, slows employment growth in what were once the booming economies of Southern California and Arizona. Environmental issues, such as acid rain and air and water pollution, emerge as important international and domestic crises.

JOB CREATION AND LABOR SHORTAGES

CHANGE 7: **New jobs will be created at the rate of 1 to 2 million each year, with some boom years resulting in the creation of more than 3 million jobs each year.**

The good news is that employment will increase in most occupations during the coming decade with export industries leading the way toward economic growth. Economic expansion in the service sector, coupled with the low productivity and low cost of labor in many parts of the service sector, contributes over 90 percent of all new jobs. Large scale manufacturing experiences labor declines while small scale manufacturing "job shops" contribute most of the minimal job growth in the manufacturing sector. The labor declines will be offset by increases in related service jobs, especially in manufacturing sales and marketing.

CHANGE 8:   **A major shortage of skilled craftspeople will create numerous production, distribution, and service problems in the coming decade.**

During the 1980s and early 1990s the number of apprenticeship programs declined significantly; fewer individuals received training in blue-collar occupations; and interest among the young in blue-collar trades declined markedly. The impact of these changes will be felt throughout the remaining 1990s and into the 21st century as production and service industries requiring critically skilled craftspeople experience major labor shortages; distribution of products and services will be uneven. Expect to personally encounter the effects of these labor shortages—long waiting periods for servicing your automobile and for repairing your home and major appliances as well as very expensive charges for such services.

AGE, RACE, SEX, AND IMMIGRANTS

CHANGE 9:   **As the baby-boomers reach retirement age and as the birth-rate continues at a near zero-population growth rate, fewer young people will be available for entry-level positions in the coming decade.**

Businesses will either recruit and train more of the hard-core unemployed, unskilled, and the elderly, and/or they will automate. As a result, more stopgap job opportunities, especially part-time minimum wage work, will be available for individuals losing their jobs or wishing to change jobs or careers.

CHANGE 10: **Retirement practices undergo a major transformation. As employers continue to downsize generous pension plans and other retirement benefits, more and more workers will continue to extend their working years. At the same time, more job and career choices will be available for the elderly who are either dissatisfied with traditional retirement or who no longer can afford the high costs of retirement.**

As the work force increasingly ages, the trend toward early retirement will decrease. Many people will never retire, preferring instead part-time or self-employment in their later years. Others will retire from one job and then start new careers after age 50. A continuing financial crisis in the social security system results in declining social security benefits. Fewer social security benefits and higher costs of retirement will further transform retirement practices and systems throughout the 1990s. Expect to see more elderly working in the McDonald's and 7-Eleven stores of tomorrow.

CHANGE 11: **More Afro-Americans and Hispanics—due to their disproportionately high birth rates, low education and skill levels, and immigration—will enter and dominate the job market at the lowest skill and wage levels.**

A large proportion of minorities will occupy the less skilled entry-level, service positions where they will exhibit marked language, class, and cultural differences. Upwardly mobile minorities may find advancement opportunities blocked because of the glut of supervisors, managers, and executives already in most organizations. Affirmative action programs continue to come under attack as detrimental to the productivity of both industry and government.

CHANGE 12: **Women will continue to enter the labor market, accounting for nearly 80 percent female participation in the coming decade.**

The entry of women into the work force during the coming decade will be due less to the changing role of women than to the economic necessity of women to generate family income in order to survive in an expensive consumer-oriented society. Women will account for two-thirds of the growth in all occupations. They will continue to expand into non-traditional jobs, especially production and management positions. Both men and women in a growing number of two-career families will have greater flexibility to change jobs and careers frequently.

CHANGE 13: **More immigrants will enter the U.S.—both documented and undocumented—to meet labor shortages at all levels.**

Despite major efforts of the INS to stem the flow of illegal immigrants, labor market demands will require more immigrants to occupy low-paying, entry-level service jobs in the 1990s. The brain drain of highly skilled scientific and technical workers from developing countries to the U.S. will accelerate. Unskilled immigrants will move into service positions vacated by upwardly mobile Americans.

PART-TIME AND WHITE-COLLAR EMPLOYMENT

CHANGE 14: **Part-time and temporary employment opportunities will increase.**

With the increase in two-career families, the continuing growth of electronic cottages, and the smaller number of retirees, part-time and temporary employment will become a more normal pattern of employment for millions of Americans. More women, who wish to enter the job market but not as full-time employees, will seek new part-time employment opportunities. Temporary employment services will experience a boom in business as more and more companies attempt to lower personnel costs as well as achieve greater personnel flexibility by hiring larger numbers of temporary employees.

CHANGE 15: **White-collar employment will continue to expand in the fast growing service sector.**

Dramatic growth in clerical and service jobs will take place in response to new information technology. The classification of workers into blue and white-collar occupations, as well as into manufacturing and service jobs, will become meaningless in a service economy dominated by white-collar workers.

EDUCATION AND UNION MEMBERSHIP

CHANGE 16: **The need for a smarter work force with specific technical skills will continue to impact on the traditional American education system as both businesses and parents demand greater job and career relevance in educational curriculum.**

Four-year colleges and universities will face stable to declining enrollments as well as the flight of quality faculty to more challenging and lucrative jobs outside education. Declining enrollments will be due to the inability of these institutions to adjust to the educational and training skill requirements of the high-tech society as well as to the demographics of fewer numbers in the traditional 18-21 year-old student age population. The flight of quality faculty will be replaced by less qualified and inexpensive part-time faculty. Most community college, as well as specialized private vocational-technical institutions, will adapt to the changing demographics and labor market needs and flourish with programs most responsive to community employment needs. As declining enrollments, budgetary crises, and flight of quality faculty accelerates, many of the traditional four-year colleges and universities will shut down or attempt to limit the educational scope of community colleges in heated state political struggles for survival of traditional educational programs. More and more emphasis will be placed on providing efficient short-term, intensive skills training programs than on providing traditional degree programs—especially in the liberal arts. Career planning will become a major emphasis in education programs; a new emphasis will be placed on specialization and flexibility in career preparation.

CHANGE 17: **Union membership will continue to decline as more blue-collar manufacturing jobs disappear and interest in unions wanes among both blue and white-collar employees.**

As unions attempt to survive and adjust to the new society, labor-management relations will go through a turbulent period of conflict, co-optation, and cooperation. Given declining union membership and the threat to lay-off employees unless unions agree to give-back arrangements, unions will continue to find themselves on the defensive, with little choice other than to agree to management demands for greater worker productivity. In the long-run, labor-management relations will shift from the traditional adversarial relationship to one of greater cooperation and participation of labor and management in the decision-making process. Profit sharing, employee ownership, Total Quality Management, and labor-management teams will become prominent features of labor-management relations. These changes will contribute to the continuing decline, and eventual disappearance, of traditional unions in many industries. New organizational forms, such as private law firms specializing in the representation of employees' interests and the negotiation of employment contracts, will replace the traditional unions.

SUBURBANISM AND REGIONALISM

CHANGE 18: **The population will continue to move into suburban and semi-rural communities as new high-tech industries and services move in this direction.**

The large, older central cities, especially in the Northeast and North Central regions, will continue to decline as well as bear disproportionate welfare and tax burdens due to their declining industrial base, deteriorating infrastructure, and relatively poor and unskilled populations. Cutbacks in their city government programs will require the retraining of public employees for private sector jobs. Urban populations will continue to move into suburban and semi-rural communities. Developing their own economic base, these communities will provide employment for the majority of local residents rather than serve as bedroom communities from which workers commute to the central city. With few exceptions, and despite noble attempts to "revitalize" downtown areas with new office, shopping, and entertainment complexes, most large central cities will continue to decline as their upwardly mobile residential populations move to the suburbs where they find good jobs, housing, and education and enjoy attractive lifestyles.

CHANGE 19: **The population, as well as wealth and economic activity, will continue to shift into the Northwest, Southwest, and Florida at the expense of the Northeast and North Central regions.**

By the year 2000 the South and West will have about 60 percent of the U.S. population. These areas will also be the home for the nation's youngest population.

Florida, Georgia, Texas, Arizona, Nevada, Colorado, Utah, and Washington will be the growth states of the 1990s; construction and local government in these states will experience major employment increases. Massachusetts, Michigan, Ohio, Illinois, Indiana, and Pennsylvania and most states in the Northeast will be in for continuing difficult times due to their declining industrial base, excessive welfare burdens, older population, aging infrastructure, and shrinkage of non-cyclical economic sectors—services, retail trade, and public employment. However, regions of several Northeast and Midwest states will experience a strong recovery due to important linkages developing between their exceptionally well developed higher educational institutions and high-tech industries which depend on such institutions. Many manufacturing industries in the Midwest, especially auto, will continue to recover as they play an increasingly important role in the expanding U.S. export economy. Indeed, many parts of the Midwest and Northwest will out-perform the rest of the economy during the second half of the 1990s.

The growth regions also will experience turbulence as they see-saw between shortages of skilled labor, surpluses of unskilled labor, and urban growth problems. A "unique event"—a devastating earthquake in Southern California or major water shortages in California and Arizona—could result in a sudden reversal of economic and employment growth in the Southwest region.

The problems of the declining regions are relatively predictable: they will become an economic drain on the nation's scarce resources; tax dollars from the growth areas will be increasingly transferred for nonproductive support payments. A new regionalism, characterized by numerous regional political conflicts, will likely arise centered around questions concerning the inequitable distribution of public costs and benefits.

SMALL BUSINESSES
AND ENTREPRENEURSHIP

CHANGE 20: **The number of small businesses will continue to increase as new opportunities for entrepreneurs arise in response to the high-tech and service revolutions and as more individuals find new opportunities to experiment with changing careers.**

Over 700,000 new businesses will be started each year during the coming decade. These businesses will generate 90 percent of all new jobs created each year. The number of business failures will increase accordingly, especially during the bust cycles of the boom/bust economy. Increases in self-employment and small businesses will not provide many new opportunities for career advancement. The small promotion hierarchies of these businesses will help accelerate increased job-hopping and career changes. This new entrepreneurship is likely to breed greater innovation, competition, and productivity.

CHANGE 21: **As large companies continue to "downsize," major job growth will take place among small companies and millions of new start-up businesses.**

Between 1980 and 1990, Fortune 500 companies reduced their personnel by 3.4 million while firms with fewer than 500 employees generated 13 million new jobs. This trend will continue throughout the 1990s and into the 21st century. The best employment opportunities in terms of challenges, salaries, and advancement opportunities will be found among growing companies employing fewer than 500 employees. Large Fortune 500 companies, especially service industries, will continue to cut jobs as they attempt to survive intense competition by becoming more productive through the application of new technology to the work place and through the introduction of more efficient management systems. Cutbacks will further lower the morale of remaining employees who will seek new job and career opportunities—and many will start their own businesses.

CAREER ADVANCEMENT AND JOB SATISFACTION

CHANGE 22: **Opportunities for career advancement will be increasingly limited within most organizations.**

Many large organizations will have difficulty providing career advancement for employees due to (1) the growth of small businesses with short advancement hierarchies, (2) the postponement of retirement, (3) the continuing focus on nonhierarchical forms of organization, and (4) the already glutted managerial ranks. During the coming decade, many of today's managers will have to find nonmanagerial positions. Job satisfaction will become less oriented toward advancement up the organizational ladder and more toward such organizational perks as club memberships, sabbaticals, vacations, retraining opportunities, flexible working hours, and family services.

CHANGE 23: **Job satisfaction will become a major problem as many organizations will experience difficulty in retaining highly qualified personnel.**

Greater competition, fewer promotions, frustrated expectations, greater discontent, and job-hopping will arise in executive ranks due to limited advancement opportunities. Managerial and executive turnover will increase accordingly. The problem will be especially pronounced for many women and minorities who have traditional aspirations to advance to the top but who will be blocked by the glut of managers and executives from the baby-boom generation. Many of these frustrated individuals will become entrepreneurs by starting their own businesses in competition with their former employers.

HIRING PRACTICES AND JOB-HOPPING

CHANGE 24: **Many employers will resort to new and unorthodox hiring practices, improved working conditions, and flexible benefit packages in order to recruit and retain critical personnel.**

In an increasingly tight job market for skilled workers, employers will use new and more effective ways of finding and keeping personnel: job fair weekends; headhunters and executive search firms; temporary employment services; on-line employment services; raids of competition's personnel; bonuses to present employees for finding needed personnel; entry-level bonuses for new recruits; attractive profit-sharing packages for long-term commitments; vacation and travel packages; relocation and housing services; flex-time and job-sharing; home-based work; and day care services.

CHANGE 25: **Job-hopping will increase as more and more individuals learn how to change careers.**

As more job and career opportunities become available for the skilled and savvy worker, as pension systems become more portable, and as job search and relocation techniques become more widely known, more and more individuals will change jobs and careers in the decade ahead. The typical employee will work in one job and organization for four years and then move on to a similar job in another organization. Within 12 years this individual will have acquired new interests and skills and thus decide to change to a new career. Similar four and 12-year cycles of job and career changes will be repeated by the same individual. Job-hopping will become an accepted and necessary way of getting ahead in the job and career markets of tomorrow.

IMPLICATIONS FOR NETWORKING

While many individuals look toward the future with unquestioned optimism, there are good reasons to be cautious and less than enthusiastic. The coming decade may be the worst of times for many people, jobs, and industries. Take several examples which indicate a need to be cautiously optimistic. Yesterday's hottest growing industries (high-tech and health care) may be tomorrow's most troubled industries. Workers who remain unemployed after five years may receive a workplace death sentence of continuing unemployment, underemployment, or socio-economic decline. Many of the poor and unskilled, with high birth rates, are destined to remain at the bottom of society; their children may fare no better. Large cities in the Northeast and North Central regions and California, and even small communities in these and other regions, will have difficult adjustment, if not survival, problems. Energy and environmental problems still remain unresolved with major implications for economic and employment growth.

The best of times are when you are gainfully employed, enjoy your work, and look to your future with optimism. In the turbulent society, people experience both the best and worst of times at the same time. Those who are unprepared for the growing uncertainty and instability of the turbulent society may get hurt.

We lack a healthy sense of reality in facing change. Indeed, the future is seldom what we think it is. Only recently have we begun to take a second look at the high-tech and service revolutions and raised some sobering questions about their impact on work and the workplace. We have not fully explored unanticipated consequences of new structural changes for individuals and society.

The 25 changes we forecast will create dislocations for individuals, groups, organizations, communities, and regions. These dislocations will require some form of public-private intervention. For example, the question of renewable energy resources has not been adequately dealt with in relation to the high-tech revolution. Many of the key metals for fueling the high-tech economy are located in politically unstable regions of Africa as well as in the former Soviet Union. Such resources must be secured or substitutions found in order for the revolution to proceed according to optimistic predictions. Capital formation, investment, and world markets must also be secure and stable. New management systems must evolve in response to the changes. In other words, the key factors are variables or "if's," and not the constants underlying most predictions of the future. As such, these are unpredictable variables which have major implications for economic growth and employment.

A clearer picture of unanticipated consequences of technological changes is already evident on the changing assembly lines, in the automated offices, and in the electronic cottages of today. While automation often creates more jobs as it displaces workers—usually at higher skill levels—the jobs may be psychologically and financially less rewarding. Supervising robots eight hours a day can be tedious and boring work with few on-the-job rewards. The same is true for the much touted "office of the future." Interacting at a work station with a computer terminal and screen eight hours a day is work that many may find tedious, tiring, and boring; and job burnout may accelerate.

The electronic cottage has similar unanticipated consequences. Many people may miss the daily interaction with fellow workers—the gossip, the politics, the strokes. Instead of being rewarding, work at home can become drudgery. It also may be low paying work—a 21st century version of the sweat shop.

The optimists often neglect the fact that the nature of work itself provides rewards. Many people intrinsically enjoy the particular job they perform. Furthermore, many rewards are tied to the human dimension of work—the interaction with others. Thus, the high-tech and service society will have to deal with serious management and motivational problems arising from the changing nature of work and the workplace.

The coming changes in the nature of work and the workplace argue for a greater emphasis on networking for finding jobs and changing careers in the decade ahead. Indeed, we see four additional changes relating to the role of networking in the job market:

CHANGE 26: **Networking plays an increasingly important role in the employment process for both employers and job seekers.**

Communication of vacancy information continues to be a major problem in the employment process due to the extreme decentralization and fragmentation of the job market. As competition becomes high for many positions and fewer qualified candidates are available for other positions, both employers and job seekers rely more and more on networking to identify qualified candidates and communicate qualifications to employers. Increased networking will be evident in both the more traditional word-of-mouth channels (information interviews and referrals) and newer electronic forms (computerized job banks and online employment services).

CHANGE 27: **Job finding organizations, from part-time employment agencies to executive search firms, play an increasingly important role in the employment process. They also increase the amount of networking taking place in the job market.**

Intermediaries between employers and candidates, such as employment agencies, temporary employment firms, headhunters, and executive search firms, encounter difficulties finding qualified candidates for their clients. As a result, they increasingly use networking strategies for finding qualified individuals. Most are forced into the electronic age by either developing or using new computerized job banks which, in effect, create new electronic networking arenas. Involving thousands of job seekers and employers who enroll as members, subscribers, or pay retainer fees, these networks operate to quickly match candidates to employers through the use of search and retrieval software designed for scanning resumes. Some even do psychological profiling and conduct pre-screening interviews on-line.

CHANGE 28: **New forms and mediums of networking play a major role in the job finding and recruitment processes during the coming decade.**

The coming decade will witness a dramatic increase in the use of electronic networking for finding jobs and recruiting candidates. Networking will increasingly be controlled by employers who discover the cost effectiveness of electronic networking in the employment process. Computer bulletin boards, electronic resume banks and databases, e-mail systems, and other electronic communication channels will help broaden the scope of hiring as well as shorten the time between when positions become vacant and qualified candidates are identified, interviewed, and hired. Computers, modems, telephones, and faxes become more acceptable and efficient mediums for networking than the traditional and extremely time consuming face-to-face meeting. More and more networking takes place impersonally through these rapidly developing and increasingly sophisticated communication mediums. Many traditional executive search firms may be threatened by the cost effective use of electronic networking for recruiting hard-to-find personnel.

CHANGE 29: **Candidates and employers alike find networking to be the preferred way to deal with mutual employment needs.**

Both interpersonal and electronic networking take center stage in the employment process as more and more individuals and organizations learn the value of networking by practicing its most effective forms on a regular basis. What was once considered to be a vague concept used by a few clever job seekers and employers seeking the "inside track" now becomes an acceptable practice for resolving many communication problems inherent in the traditional job market. Best of all, networking becomes the most cost-effective way of linking qualified candidates to employers.

More and more individuals will change jobs and careers in order to overcome the boredom and burnout accompanying many of the new jobs or work situations of tomorrow. The major source and method for making job and career changes will be your networks and networking activities. If practiced properly, networks and networking will quickly generate information, advice, job leads, and invitations to interview in an increasingly chaotic job market. In this new job market, "who you know" and "who knows you" are just as important to getting a job and advancing your career as your ability to "do the job."

3

NETWORKS, NETWORKING, AND YOUR JOB SEARCH

What exactly are networks and the process of networking, and how do they affect you and your job search? These questions are central to any discussion of finding jobs and advancing careers in today's job market. Clear and practical answers to these questions provide the basic foundation from which you can develop your own successful networking activities.

THE FOUR NETWORKS

Not surprising, there are as many different definitions of networks as there are examples of networks. For our purposes we define and illustrate networks at four important levels in the job search process: the individual, organization, community, and electronic. If you want to be successful in your job search, you must be aware of all four levels of networks as well as know how each level is linked to the other. Distinctions among these levels are necessary simply because most individuals simultaneously function at all four levels. You are, for example, an individual when you deal with other individuals. However, you also deal with organizations, and individuals and organizations are the building blocks of communities which, in turn, make up societies. You may also participate in an electronic network which provides information and contacts relevant to finding a job.

If you wish to move from one community to another—conduct a "long-distance" job search—you should be aware that the networks of individuals must be linked to networks of organizations that define opportunities in communities. Electronic networks may play a key role in conducting an effective long-distance job search. These distinctions and linkages will become clearer as we further define networks through several illustrations and examples.

INDIVIDUAL LEVEL NETWORKS

At the **individual level**, your network is your interpersonal environment. It consists of individuals you know, who are important to you, and with whom you interact at different times and occasions. Many of the people you interact with most frequently have a major influence on your behavior. Other individuals may also influence your behavior, but you interact with them less frequently. While you may know and interact with hundreds of people, on a day-to-day basis you probably encounter no more than 20 people.

The figure on page 38 outlines a hypothetical network which we will again refer to in Chapter 5 when we begin identifying your own network. For now, this network consists of people with whom you have frequent contact in face-to-face situations. Within your network, some people are more important to you than others. You like some more than others. And some will be more helpful to you in your job search and advancement than others. Your basic network will most likely encompass the follow-

YOUR NETWORK OF RELATIONSHIPS

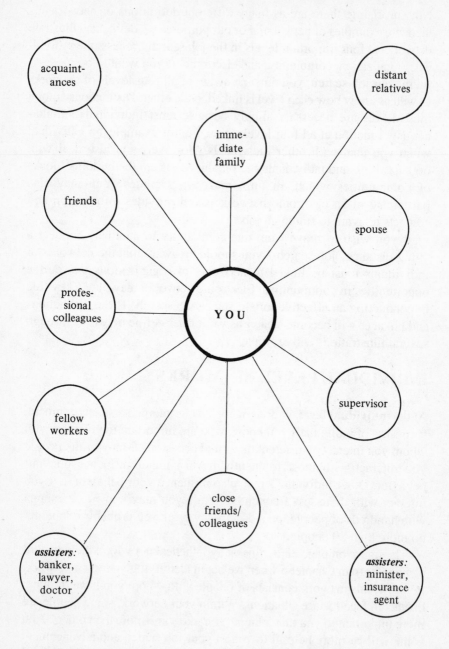

ing individuals and groups: friends, acquaintances, immediate family, distant relatives, professional colleagues, spouse, supervisor, fellow workers, close friends, mentor, and local business people and professionals, such as your banker, lawyer, doctor, minister, and insurance agent. These individuals will play a central role in your networking activities, the process by which you activate your network for specific job and career purposes.

ORGANIZATIONAL LEVEL NETWORKS

At the **organizational level**, networks consist of interacting positions, groups, offices, departments, and other organizational subdivisions and units that define both the formal and informal structure of an organization. Examples of typical elements defining an organization's network are supervisor, personnel office, planning unit, training office, and committees. As illustrated on page 40, these elements interact in defining the unique structure of most organizations. They also link one organization to another. They are a few of many contact points toward which individuals target their organizational networking activities. Organizational networks also include important **professional associations** that function both inside and outside organizations. As again illustrated in the figure on page 38, personnel officers or training personnel from thousands of different organizations, for example, may be members of one or two national personnel associations that publish newsletters and journals, hold local chapter meetings and annual conferences, and operate job placement activities. Many members of these associations use them as forums for making professional contacts, building networks, and changing jobs and careers when necessary. Such organizations become key mechanisms for linking, building, and expanding networks across organizations.

The role of professional associations in linking personnel from one organization to another challenge popular notions of loyalty to a single organization. Professional associations tend to emphasize professional competence and loyalty to one's profession. In such an organizational situation, job and career advancement takes place through the process of networking for jobs in different organizations which have similar professional positions. Loyalty to one's professional association often takes precedence over commitment to one's current job in any one particular organization.

At the organizational level, an individual's network therefore consists

ORGANIZATIONAL NETWORKS

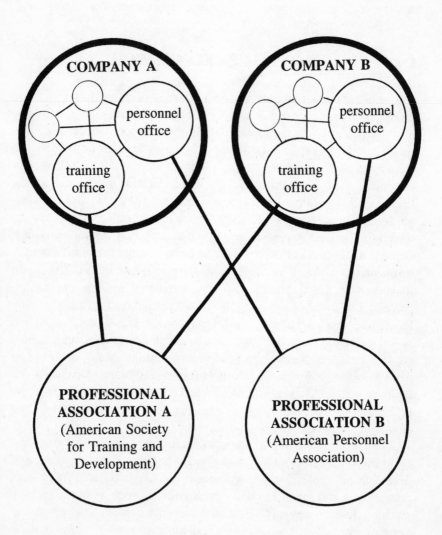

of much more than those individuals they interact with on a daily basis. Their organizational level of networks consists of **opportunity structures**, such as professional associations, that enable them to link and expand their networks into other organizations with relative ease.

COMMUNITY LEVEL NETWORKS

At the **community level**, networks consist of different organizations that define the structure of communities and enable individuals to gain access to new job and career opportunities through the combined processes of individual, organizational, and community networking. Each community, for example, has its own social, economic, political, and job market structure. The degree of structure differs for every community. However, one thing is relatively predictable: **most communities lack a coherent structure for processing job information efficiently and effectively**. Identifying these organizations and knowing how they interact with each other is key to making a **long-distance job search** in an unfamiliar community where standard networking strategies designed primarily at the individual level may or may not function well in reference to the local power structure.

Let's illustrate this level of networks with a few examples. Each community is made up of numerous individuals, groups, organizations, and institutions that are involved in pursuing their own interests in both cooperation and competition with one another. The Yellow Pages of your telephone book best outline the major actors. Banks, mortgage companies, advertising firms, car dealers, schools, churches, small businesses, industries, hospitals, law firms, governments, and civic and voluntary groups do their "own thing" and have their own internal power structure. No one dominates except in small communities which also may be company towns—mills, mining companies, publishing firms, universities, aerospace, and the military. At the same time, the groups overlap with each other because of economic, political, social, and professional needs. The bank, for example, needs to loan money to the businesses and churches. The businesses, in turn, need the educational institutions. And the educational institutions need the businesses to absorb their graduates. Therefore, individuals tend to cooperate to ensure that people playing the other games also succeed. Members of school boards, medical boards, and the boardrooms of banks and corporations will overlap and give the appearance of a "power structure" even though power is structured in the loosest sense of the term. The players in this game compete and cooperate with each other as well as co-op one another. The structures they create can become **your opportunity structures for penetrating the hidden job market.**

Take the example of Washington, DC. The opportunity structures for your job search networks at all three levels—community, organizational, and individual—are relatively well defined in this city. While government is the major institution, other institutions are also well defined in relation to the government. Within government, both the political and administrative institutions function as alternative opportunity structures in the Washington networks: congressional staffs, congressional committees, congressional subcommittees, congressional bureaucracy, executive staff, departments, independent executive agencies, and independent regulatory agencies. Outside, but clinging to, government are a variety of other groups and networks: interest groups, the media, professional associations, contractors, consultants, law firms, banks, and universities and colleges. As illustrated on page 43, these groups are linked to one another for survival and advancement. Charles Peters (*How Washington Really Works*) calls them "survival networks" which function in the "make believe world" of Washington, DC. Ripley and Franklin (*Congress, Bureaucracy, and Public Policy*) identify the key political dynamics as "subgovernments"—the interaction of interest groups, agencies, and congressional committees. For the purposes of finding jobs and advancing careers, we call these your "**opportunity structures**" for getting ahead in the community regardless of its location.

For years Washington insiders have learned how to use these "opportunity structures" to advance their careers. They illustrate how networks at the individual, organizational, and community level are used simultaneously for getting jobs and advancing careers. A frequent career pattern might be to work in an agency for three to four years. During that time, one would make important contacts on Capitol Hill with congressional staffs and committees as well as with private consultants, contractors, and interest groups. One's specialized knowledge on the inner workings of government is marketable to these other people. Therefore, it is relatively easy to make a job change from a federal agency to a congressional committee or to an interest group. After a few years here, you move to another group in the network. Perhaps you work on your law degree at the same time so that in another five years you can go into the truly growth industry in the city—law firms. The keys to making these moves are the personal contacts—whom you know—and networking. Particular attention is given to keeping a current SF-171 (federal government's application form) or resume, just in case an opportunity

COMMUNITY LEVEL NETWORKS AS OPPORTUNITY STRUCTURES FOR WASHINGTON, DC

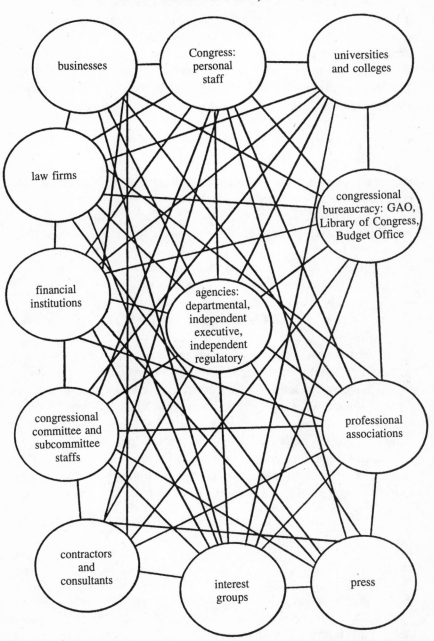

happens to come your way. Congressional staff members usually last no more than two years; they set their sights on consulting and contracting firms, agencies, or interest groups for their next job move.

Whatever community you decide to focus your job search on, expect it to have its particular networks. Do as much research as possible to identify the structure of the networks as well as the key people who can provide access to various elements in the opportunity structures. Washington is not unique in this respect; it is just better known, and Washingtonians talk about it more because of their frequent job moves and their constant use of networking strategies for finding employment.

ELECTRONIC NETWORKS

Electronic networks help integrate individual, organizational, and community networks. A recent and rapidly evolving innovation in the employment business, electronic networks include several computerized membership-based groups—also known as computerized job or resume banks—which are designed to quickly link candidates to employers through the use of search and retrieval computer software. Joining one of these networks enables users to gain access to hundreds of nationwide employers. The major operators of such networks include Career Net Graduate, Cors, Job Bank USA, National Resume Bank, SkillSearch, and University ProNet. Other electronic job search options include a variety of job search services operated through online commercial services, such as America Online, CompuServe, and Prodigy, or on the Internet via the World Wide Web (Online Career Center, CareerWeb, Career Mosiac, E-Span's Interactive Employment Network). Many of these services include bulletin boards, discussion groups, and e-mail for acquiring career counseling, identifying job vacancies, posting resumes, and networking for information, advice, and referrals. Chapter 9 outlines these and other electronic networks that are transforming today's job market as well as adding a new dimension to traditional job search and networking strategies.

NETWORKING

Networking is both a technique and a process centered around specific goals. As a technique, networking involves purposefully developing relations with others. Networking as a job search technique involves connecting and interacting with other individuals by means of prospecting, networking, and informational interviewing. Its purpose is to exchange information and acquire advice and referrals that will assist you in promoting your ultimate job search goal—getting job interviews and offers. Through the process of networking you build, expand, and activate your networks:

TECHNIQUES, PROCESSES, AND GOALS OF NETWORKING

Techniques	Processes	Goals
Prospecting	Identifying and building networks	Develop a networking strategy
Networking	Linking and expanding networks	Establish contacts that lead to infor- mational interviews
Informational interviews	Networking to achieve goals	Acquire key infor- mation, advice, and referrals that will lead to job inter- views and offers

The process of networking involves both identifying your own networks (page 38) as well as linking your networks to the networks of others. As illustrated on page 46, you expand your network by linking it to the networks of other individuals who also have job information and contacts. Through the process of networking, you ask people in your basic network for referrals to individuals in their networks. This approach will greatly enlarge your basic job search network.

Examples of networking abound within the job search. You are interested in learning about job opportunities with XYZ Company, but you don't know anyone who works there. You ask a friend if she knows anyone who works for XYZ Company. She, in turn, refers you to John

LINKING YOUR NETWORKS TO OTHERS

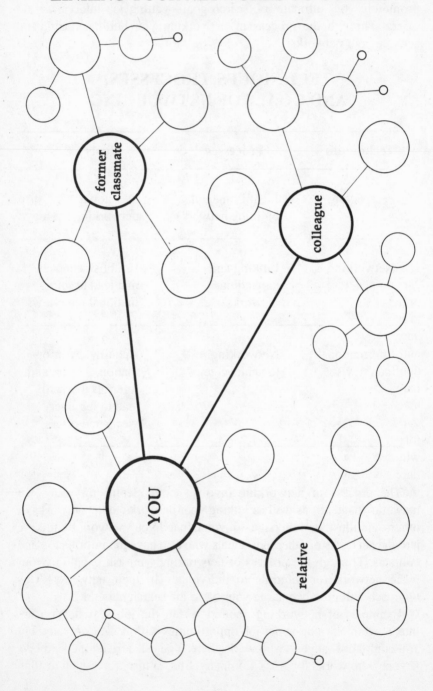

Taylor who retired from XYZ company two years ago. You call John Taylor and mention that your friend suggested that you give him a call because he was someone who might be able to provide you with information on XYZ Company. You meet with John Taylor and learn a great deal about the internal operations of the company. In addition, John Taylor provides you with the names of three individuals who presently work at XYZ Company and who would be willing to talk to you about your career interests. You contact these individuals, conduct informational interviews with them, and begin gaining access to the hidden job market within the company. This process continues as you receive additional referrals to individuals within the company who know about job vacancies and who make hiring decisions.

Take another example to illustrate how this might work in the case of a **long-distance job search**. You may live in Indianapolis, Indiana and wish to relocate to Orlando, Florida. While you know a great deal about Florida and living in Orlando (cost of living, housing, community activities, recreational opportunities), you know little about job and career opportunities there. In need of conducting a long-distance job campaign, you wonder how you can find a job in Orlando while living in Indianapolis. You first begin by subscribing to the Orlando newspaper to survey the "Help Wanted" section of the classifieds and respond to job vacancy announcements that seem appropriate to your skills, interests, and experience. However, after receiving no encouraging replies, you decide it's time to begin conducting a long-distance networking campaign. You begin doing this by contacting your university alumni association at Ohio State University for names of alumni who now live in the Orlando area and who would be willing to talk to you about your job and career interests. They provide you with a list of six graduates whom you contact by letter and telephone. They indicate they will be happy to assist you with information, advice, and referrals. Since these individuals have moved into prominent positions within the community, their information, advice, and referrals appear to be invaluable to your job search. After contacting these individuals and their referrals by letter and telephone, you decide it is now time to visit Orlando for 10 days to further expand your newly developed Orlando networks. During your 10-day visit, you further expand your network by meeting with 33 individuals who provide you with more information, advice, and referrals. During this time you also conduct two job interviews based on newly acquired referrals. The one interview results in a job offer, which you accept. You now return to Indianapolis to make arrangements for moving to Orlando within the next two months.

ADVERTISED AND HIDDEN
JOB MARKETS

Networks and networking play a central role in finding jobs and changing careers because of the particular structure of the job market. The so-called "job market" actually consists of two structurally different arenas for locating job opportunities—one advertised and another hidden. Both are characterized by a high degree of decentralization, fragmentation, and chaos. Neither should be underestimated nor overestimated when conducting a job search.

The **advertised job market** consists of job vacancy announcements and listings found in newspapers, professional and trade journals, newsletters as well as through employment agencies and personnel offices. With the recent development of electronic employment resources, many employers now prefer posting vacancy announcements with electronic job banks and on-line career services in addition to, or in lieu of, these traditional print sources and service centers. Indeed, these electronic sources, which constitute a new advertised job market, potentially threaten the future viability of the traditional advertised job market.

Most people focus on this advertised job market because it is relatively easy to find, and because they believe it accurately reflects available job vacancies at any given moment. In reality, however, the advertised job market probably represents no more than 25 percent of actual job openings. Furthermore, this market tends to represent positions at the extreme ends of the job spectrum—low-paying unskilled or high-paying highly skilled jobs. The majority of positions lying between these two extremes are not well represented in the listings. Competition often is great for the low and middle-level positions. Worst of all, many of these advertised jobs are either nonexistent or are filled prior to the appearance of the ad.

You should spend a minimum amount of time looking for employment in the advertised job markets. Monitor this market, but don't assume it represents the entire spectrum of job opportunities. Your job search time and money are better spent elsewhere—on the hidden job market. When you identify an advertised position that is right for you, send a cover letter and resume and follow-up with a telephone call—but keep moving on to other potential opportunities.

However, you will find exceptions to this general rule of avoiding the advertised job market. Each occupational specialty has its own internal recruitment and job finding structure. Some occupations are represented more by professional listing and recruitment services than others. Indeed, as we increasingly become a high-tech society, greater efforts will be made by both government and the private sector to increase the efficiency of employment communication by centralizing listings and recruitment services for particular occupational specialties. These services will be designed to reduce the **lag time** between when a job becomes vacant and is filled. Computerized job banks and on-line career centers with recruitment and employment capabilities will increasingly be used by employers to locate qualified candidates, and vice versa. Employers in a high-tech society need to reduce lag time as much as possible given the increasing interdependency of positions in high-tech industries. If and when such employment services and job banks become available for your occupational specialty, you should at least investigate them. In the meantime, since the job market will remain relatively disorganized in the foreseeable future, do your research and use job search strategies, such as networking, which are appropriate for this type of job market.

Your research should center on one of the key dynamics to finding employment—helping employers solve their hiring problems. Many employers turn to the advertised job market **after** they fail to recruit candidates by other, less formal and public, means. The lag time between when a position becomes vacant, is listed, and then filled is a critical period for your attention and **intervention with networking strategies**. Your goal should be to locate high quality job vacancies before they are listed.

The **hidden job market** is where the action is. It is this job market that should occupy most of your attention. Although this job market lacks a formal structure, 75 percent or more of all job opportunities are found here. Your task is to give this market some semblance of structure and coherence so that you can effectively penetrate it. If you can do this, the hidden job market will yield numerous job interviews and offers that should be right for you.

Networking is the key to penetrating the hidden job market. Consider, for example, the hiring problems of employers by putting yourself in their place. Suppose one of your employees suddenly gives you a two week notice, or you terminate someone. Now you have a problem—you must hire a new employee. It takes time and it is a risky business you would prefer to avoid. After hours of reading resumes and interviewing, you still will be hiring an unknown who might create new problems for you.

Like many other employers, you want to **minimize your time and risks**. You can do this by networking with your friends and acquaintances—contacting them to let them know you are looking for someone; you would appreciate it if they could **refer** some good candidates to you. Based on these contacts, you should receive referrals. At the same time, you want to hedge your bets, as well as fulfill affirmative action and equal opportunity requirements, by listing the job vacancy in the newspaper, with your personnel office, or through an on-line employment service. While 300 people respond by mail to your classified ad, you also get referrals from the trusted individuals in your network. In the end, you conduct 10 telephone interviews and three face-to-face interviews. You hire the **best** candidate—the one your former classmate recommended to you on the first day you informed her of your need to fill the vacancy. You are satisfied with your excellent choice of candidates; you are relatively certain this new employee will be a good addition to your organization.

This scenario is played out regularly in many organizations. In fact, some companies institutionalize this networking process by offering employees "finder fees" for referring qualified candidates to the company. It demonstrates the importance of getting into the interpersonal networks of the hidden job market and devoting most of your time and energy there. If you let people know you are looking for employment, chances are they will keep you in mind and refer you to others who may have an unexpected vacancy. Your networking activities will help you enter and maneuver within this job market of interpersonal networks and highly personalized information exchanges.

FINDING JOBS AND CHANGING CAREERS

If you are looking for your first job, reentering the job market after a lengthy absence, or planning a job or career change, you will join an army of millions of individuals who do so each year. Indeed, more than 15 million people find themselves unemployed each year. Millions of others try to increase their satisfaction within the workplace as well as advance their careers by looking for alternative jobs and careers. If you are like most other Americans, you will make more than 10 job changes and between 3 and 5 career changes during your lifetime.

Most people make job or career transitions by accident. They do little other than take advantage of opportunities that may arise unexpectedly.

While chance and luck do play important roles in finding employment, we recommend that you plan for future job and career changes so that you will experience even greater degrees of chance and luck!

Finding a job or changing a career in a systematic and well-planned manner is hard yet rewarding work. The task should first be based upon a clear understanding of the key ingredients that define jobs and careers. Starting with this understanding, you should next convert key concepts into action steps for implementing your job search.

A career is a series of related jobs which have common skill, interest, and motivational bases. You may change jobs several times without changing careers. But once you change skills, interests, and motivations, you change careers.

It's not easy to find a job given the present structure of the job market. You will find the job market to be relatively disorganized, although it projects an outward appearance of coherence. If you seek comprehensive, accurate, and timely job information, the job market will frustrate you with its poor communication. While you will find many employment services ready to assist you, such services tend to be fragmented and their performance is often disappointing. Job search methods are controversial and many are ineffective. Even the much hyped new electronic job banks and on-line career services have yet to demonstrate their effectiveness.

No system is organized to give people jobs. At best you will encounter a decentralized and fragmented system consisting of job listings in newspapers, trade journals, employment offices, or computerized job banks—all designed to link potential candidates with available job openings. Many people will try to sell you job information as well as questionable job search services. While efforts are underway to create a nationwide computerized job bank (America's Job Bank) that would list available job vacancies on a daily basis, don't expect such data to become available soon nor to be very useful for your particular employment situation. Many of the listed jobs may be nonexistent, at a low skill and salary level, or represent only a few employers. In the end, most of the systems organized to help you find a job do not provide you with the information you need in order to land a job that is most related to your skills and interests. When looking for employment, your best friend will be you. Hopefully you will have organized a coherent job search campaign centered around networking strategies for penetrating the hidden job market.

CAREER DEVELOPMENT AND
JOB SEARCH PROCESSES

Networking plays a key role in the overall career development and job search processes. If you want to find a job or change careers, you must first know how networking relates to other equally important career development and job search steps.

Finding a job is both an art and a science; it encompasses a variety of basic facts, principles, and skills you can learn but which you must also adapt to different situations. Thus, **learning how to find a job** can be as important to career success as **knowing how to perform a job**. However, having marketable skills is essential to making job search strategies work effectively for you.

Our understanding of how to find jobs and change careers is illustrated on pages 53 and 55. As outlined on page 53, you should involve yourself in a four-step career development process as you prepare to move from one job to another:

STEP 1: Conduct a self-assessment

> This first step involves assessing your skills, abilities, motivations, interests, values, temperament, experience, and accomplishments. Your basic strategy is to develop a firm foundation of information about yourself before proceeding to other stages in the career development process. This self-assessment develops the necessary self-awareness upon which you can effectively communicate your qualifications to employers as well as focus and build your career.

STEP 2: Gather career information

> Closely related to the first step, this second step is an exploratory, research phase of your career development. Here you need to formulate goals, gather information about alternative jobs and careers through reading and talking to informed people, and then narrow your alternatives to specific job targets.

THE CAREER DEVELOPMENT PROCESS

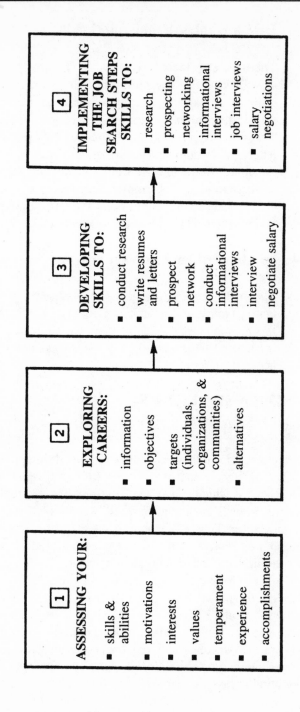

1 ASSESSING YOUR:

- skills & abilities
- motivations
- interests
- values
- temperament
- experience
- accomplishments

2 EXPLORING CAREERS:

- information
- objectives
- targets (individuals, organizations, & communities)
- alternatives

3 DEVELOPING SKILLS TO:

- conduct research
- write resumes and letters
- prospect
- network
- conduct informational interviews
- interview
- negotiate salary

4 IMPLEMENTING THE JOB SEARCH STEPS SKILLS TO:

- research
- prospecting
- networking
- informational interviews
- job interviews
- salary negotiations

STEP 3: Develop job search skills

The third step focuses your career around specific job search skills for landing the job you want. As further outlined on page 53, these job search skills are closely related to one another as a series of job search steps. They involve conducting research, writing resumes and letters, prospecting and networking, conducting informational interviews, interviewing for a job, and negotiating salary and terms of employment. Each of these job search skills involves well-defined strategies and tactics you must learn in order to be effective in the job market.

STEP 4: Implement each job search step

The final career development step emphasizes the importance of transforming understanding into action. You do this by implementing each job search step which already incorporates the knowledge, skills, and abilities you acquired in Steps 1, 2, and 3.

ORGANIZE AND SEQUENCE YOUR JOB SEARCH

The figure on page 55 further expands our career development process by examining the key elements in a successful job search. It consists of a seven-step process which relates your past, present, and future. Notice that your past is well integrated into the process of finding a job or changing your career. Therefore, you should feel comfortable conducting your job search: it represents the best of what you are in terms of your past and present accomplishments as they relate to your present and future goals. If you follow this type of job search, you will communicate your best self to employers.

Since the individual job search steps are interrelated, they should be followed in sequence. If you fail to properly complete the initial self-assessment steps, your job search may become haphazard, aimless, and costly. For example, you should never write a resume (Step 3) before first conducting an assessment of your skills (Step 1) and identifying your objective (Step 2). You normally should do networking (Step 5) after assessing your skills (Step 1), identifying your objective (Step 2),

JOB SEARCH STEPS
AND SKILLS

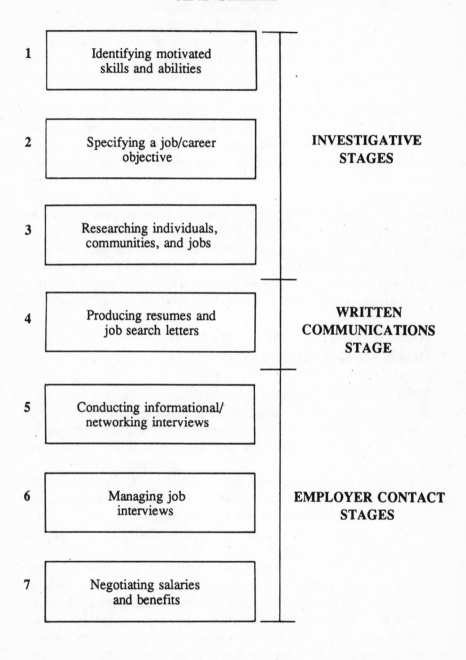

1	Identifying motivated skills and abilities	
2	Specifying a job/career objective	**INVESTIGATIVE STAGES**
3	Researching individuals, communities, and jobs	
4	Producing resumes and job search letters	**WRITTEN COMMUNICATIONS STAGE**
5	Conducting informational/ networking interviews	
6	Managing job interviews	**EMPLOYER CONTACT STAGES**
7	Negotiating salaries and benefits	

writing a resume (Step 3), and conducting research (Step 4). Indeed, relating Step 1 to Step 2 is especially critical to the successful implementation of all other job search steps. You must complete Steps 1 and 2 before continuing on to the other steps. Steps 3 to 6 can be conducted simultaneously because they complement and reinforce one another.

Try to sequence your job search as close to these steps as possible. The true value of this sequencing will become very apparent as you implement your plan.

The processes and steps identified on pages 53 and 55 represent the careering and re-careering processes we and others have used successfully with thousands of clients during the past 30 years. But this is not the complete picture on finding jobs and advancing careers in the job markets of today and tomorrow. You must do much more than just know how to find a job through networking. In the job markets of today and tomorrow, you need to constantly review your work-content skills to make sure they are appropriate for the changing job market. Once you have the necessary skills to perform jobs, you will be ready to target your skills on particular jobs and careers that you do well and enjoy doing. You will be able to avoid the trap of trying to fit into jobs that are not conducive to your particular mix of skills, motivations, and abilities.

ACHIEVING SUCCESS THROUGH PLANNING AND NETWORKING

While we recommend that you plan your job search, we want you to avoid the excesses of too much planning. Planning should not become all-consuming. Planning makes sense because it requires that you set goals and develop strategies for achieving the goals. However, too much planning can blind you to unexpected occurrences and opportunities—that wonderful experience called serendipity. Be flexible enough to take advantage of new opportunities that come your way, many of which will be generated from your networking activities.

We outline a hypothetical plan for conducting an effective job search on page 57. This plan incorporates the individual job search activities over a six month period. If you phase in the first five job search steps during the initial three to four weeks and continue the final four steps in subsequent weeks and months, you should begin receiving job offers within two to three months after initiating your job search. Interviews and job offers can come anytime—often unexpectedly—as you conduct your job search. An average time is within three months, but it can occur

ORGANIZATION OF JOB SEARCH ACTIVITIES

Activity	Weeks 1 2 3 4 5 6 7 8 9 10 11 12 13 14 15 16 17 18 19 20 21 22 23 24
• Thinking, questioning, listening evaluating, adjusting	(bar spans weeks 1–24)
• Identifying abilities & skills	(bar spans weeks 1–4)
• Setting objectives	(bar spans weeks 1–4)
• Writing resume	(bar spans weeks 1–5)
• Conducting research	(bar spans weeks 1–24)
• Prospecting, referrals, networking	(bar spans weeks 1–24)
• Interviewing	(dashed line spans weeks 9–24)
• Receiving and negotiating job offers	(dashed line spans weeks 11–24)

within a week or take as long as five months. If you plan, prepare, and persist at the job search, the pay-off will be job interviews and offers.

Networking plays a central on-going role in moving your job search to its final goals—job interviews and offers. While three months may seem a long time, especially if you have just lost your job and you need work immediately, you can shorten your job search time by increasing the frequency of your prospecting, networking, and informational interviewing activities. If you are job hunting on a full-time basis, you may be able to cut your job search time in half. But don't expect to get a job within a week or two. It requires time and hard work—perhaps the hardest work you will ever do—but it pays off with a job that is right for you.

DO YOUR HOMEWORK

One word of caution before we proceed further. An important lesson we and others have learned over the years is this:

> Effective networking and job interviewing are based upon a strong job search foundation of self-assessment, skills identification, objective setting, research, and resume/letter writing.

Don't short-change yourself by failing to do your homework. Be sure to complete each step in the job search process. If you do this, you should become a very effective networker who will find jobs that you both do well and enjoy doing.

4

MYTHS, ABUSES, AND MISUSES OF NETWORKS

Most people have an image of how the job market works as well as how they should relate to it. This image is based upon a combination of facts, stereotypes, and myths learned from experience and from the advice of well-meaning individuals. It's a useful image when it leads individuals into productive job search channels that quickly result in job interviews and offers for excellent jobs. But it's an unfortunate image when it guides people into unproductive job search channels. The image is at its worst when it advises job seekers to spend most of their time responding to vacancy announcements and waiting to hear from employers.

Such images lead job seekers into using job search approaches that often result in less than rewarding jobs. Indeed, they reconfirm the often-heard lament of the frustrated, disappointed, and unsuccessful job searcher—*"What more can I do—there are no jobs out there for me."* This should not happen to you because you are a proactive job seeker. Using networking strategies, you will take initiative to uncover numerous job leads that will result in job interviews and offers.

At the same time, there are several myths surrounding networks and networking. Like many concepts that come into vogue, this one has become the object of exaggerated claims, abuses, and misuses.

Let's examine several of these myths before you proceed to organize your networks and networking activities. Each of these myths stresses important principles for identifying, developing, expanding, and using networks and networking strategies in a job search.

JOB SEARCH AND WORK-CONTENT SKILLS

MYTH 1:   **Anyone can find a job; all you need to know is "how to find a job."**

REALITY: This "form versus substance" myth is often associated with career counselors who were raised on popular career planning exhortations of the 1970s and 1980s that stressed the importance of having positive attitudes and self-esteem, setting goals, dressing for success, and using interpersonal strategies for finding jobs. These individuals have been more concerned with promoting a job search philosophy—which emphasizes process skills—than with urging more job generation, the development of work-content skills, and relocation. It reflects a disturbing preference for style and image rather than substance and performance in the workplace. This myth was most likely a reality in an industrial society with low unemployment—the 1950s and 1960s—or in certain high turnover service sectors requiring low level skills—the 1980s. But it is a myth for the post-industrial, high-tech society of the 1990s. In a society that requires more and more highly skilled labor, knowing how to find a job is not enough to get a good job. Getting a job in such a society also requires that (1) jobs be available (job generation), (2) individuals have the proper mix of skills to perform those jobs (work-content skills), and (3) individuals be willing to go where the jobs are located (relocation). While it is extremely important to learn job search skills, these skills are no substitute for concrete work-content skills, job generation, and relocation.

FINDING JOBS

MYTH 2: **The best way to find a job is to respond to classified ads, use employment agencies, use on-line career services, submit applications, and fax, E-mail, or mail resumes and cover letters to personnel offices.**

REALITY: This is one of the most serious myths preventing many individuals from finding a good job. Many people do get jobs by following such formalized application and recruitment procedures. However, these are not the best ways to get the best jobs— those offering good pay, advancement opportunities, and an appropriate "fit" with one's abilities, goals, and values. This approach makes two questionable assumptions about the structure of the job market and how you should relate to it. The first assumption deals with how the job market does or should operate:

> **Assumption #1:** There is an organized, coherent, and centralized job market "out there" where one can go to get information on available job vacancies.

In reality no such market exists. It is a highly decentralized, fragmented, and chaotic job market where job vacancy information is at best incomplete, skewed, and unrepresentative of available job opportunities at any particular moment. Classified ads, agencies, and personnel offices tend to list low paying yet highly competitive jobs. Most of the best jobs—high level, excellent pay, least competitive—are neither listed nor advertised; they are uncovered through word-of-mouth and learned about during the process of networking. When seeking employment, your most fruitful strategy will be to conduct research and informational interviews on what is called the "hidden job market"—a loosely structured network of employers and job seekers who exchange job vacancy and hiring information.

The second assumption deals with how you should relate to this job market:

> **Assumption #2:** You should try to fit your goals and abilities into existing vacancies rather than find a job designed around your strengths.

This may be a formula for future job unhappiness. If you want to find a job fit for you rather than try to fit yourself into a job, you must use another job search strategy based upon a different set of assumptions regarding how you should relate your goals and abilities to the world of work.

MYTH 3:   **I know how to find a job but opportunities are not available for me.**

REALITY: Most people don't know how to best find a job. They may be unable to identify work-content skills to communicate their value to employers, or they look in the wrong places where jobs are not being generated. They continue to use the most ineffective methods—responding to job listings, sending resumes, contacting employment agencies, or spending a disproportionate amount of time on the computer looking for jobs online. Opportunities are readily available for those who understand the structure and operation of the job market, can identify appropriate work-content skills, are willing to relocate, and use job search methods designed for the hidden job market. Networking is the key job search strategy for penetrating the hidden job market.

MYTH 4: One should not network in a case where there is an advertised vacancy and an employer requests a resume or completed application form.

REALITY: Networking should especially be used in the case of advertised job vacancies. If you only complete an application form or submit a resume, chances are nothing will happen. You must take additional action —a telephone call or a personal visit—to assist your application. Such forms of networking can help your application and resume stand out from the rest.

INFORMATION, ADVICE, AND REFERRALS

MYTH 5: The purpose of networking is to get a job interview and job offer.

REALITY: While networking may ultimately lead to interviews and job offers, the purpose of networking is to get information, advice, and referrals so you can better identify job leads as well as communicate your qualifications to potential employers. In every step of your job search you need more and better information on which to make decisions; employers also need this information on potential candidates. You get this by talking to people who have information. If you approach networking as a method for getting job interviews and offers, you will most likely become ineffective. You may appear insincere and untrustworthy as you attempt to use people for personal gain. You must communicate that you are honest, sincere, likable, and competent. You can best communicate these qualities to others by seeking information, advice, and referrals.

MYTH 6: Networking is the key to getting a job.

REALITY: Networking is one of several **techniques** used in getting a job. It is more or less effective depending on how you use it as well as the behavior of your intended audience. Many other methods used in finding jobs have little or nothing to do with networking: complete an application form for a job vacancy; submit a letter and resume in response to a classified ad; or interview directly for a position. These more traditional methods for finding a job are most appropriate for individuals who are seeking to fit their interests, experience, and qualifications into available job vacancies found on the advertised job market. Networking is most appropriate for individuals interested in finding high quality jobs that fit more directly with their own motivated abilities and skills. These jobs are more likely to be found on the hidden job market rather than on the advertised job market. Individuals who know how to network are more likely to get job interviews that lead to job offers.

NETWORKING STRATEGIES

MYTH 7:   **Your networking activities should be aimed at those who have the power to hire.**

REALITY: This belief is responsible for many abuses and misuses of networking. This is an example of how a little knowledge can become a dangerous thing. Many people who learn about networking remain confused about where to target their networking activities. They either don't know what they are doing or they lack a clear understanding about the purpose of networking. As a result, they often engage in unproductive activities. Many, for example, believe that networking is all about acquiring "connections," power, and influence in order to "pull strings" that will help get them a job. They forget that they should be **gathering high quality information and advice** in order to make employment decisions. Consequently, they only seek out people who seem to be powerful in the hopes they will open the right doors to success. Such people often pester others who are busy and have no reasons whatsoever to meet with them. Such abuses and misuses of networking are partly due to advice given to job seekers by well-meaning but inexperienced career advisors who counsel job seekers to aim their job search activities toward those who have the power to hire. Remember, **networking is a communication process**—exchanging information and receiving advice and referrals about jobs and careers. While it involves prospecting and informational interviewing, and it should lead to job interviews and offers, don't approach networking as strictly a job finding technique. Those that do often abuse networking by contacting individuals for the ostensible purpose of gathering information, but in reality they attempt to use the individual for getting a job. By focusing on individuals who have the power to hire, they give networking a bad name by bothering busy people who do not have the time nor interest in giving these "networkers" a job. Returning to the original purposes of networking, you will find that many people who do not have the power to hire also have very valuable information, advice, and referrals to share with you as you progress in your job search. You will find, for example, that a secretary may be able to provide greater insights into an organization—especially its politics—than more influential individuals who appear to have the power to hire. Furthermore, it is not always clear who has the power to hire since **hiring decisions are often shared decisions** involving many individuals. Whatever you do, approach networking as a communication process rather than a process of acquiring power and influence with employers.

MYTH 8:   **The best way to network is to join professional associations. Members of these organizations will help you gain access to job vacancies that arise in their organizations.**

REALITY: Important networking does take place in many professional associations, but joining professional associations is by no means the best way to network. Indeed, too many people join professional associations with the mistaken impression that membership alone will enhance their job search. Some professional associations are peopled by so many "networkers" looking for jobs that many of the more established, experienced, and talented professionals avoid participating in such associations for fear of becoming the subject of networking rather than participate in an organization that promotes substantive professional goals. Furthermore, membership in any organization is only as good as one's participation in the organization. If you decide to join professional associations, the best form of networking is to become seen and known—a **participant** rather than a spectator—for your activities and competence within the organization. You should promote the goals of the organization by serving on committees, taking on assignments, and playing a significant role in monthly meetings and annual conferences. In other words, demonstrate your capabilities by becoming involved in the operations of the association rather than by collecting names, addresses, and phone numbers of fellow members for the misguided purpose of acquiring "connections" that will lead to job opportunities. **The best form of networking is one that communicates your qualifications to potential employers by demonstrating your capabilities within an organization**.

INTERPERSONAL AND ELECTRONIC NETWORKING

MYTH 9:   **Electronic networking is the wave of the future. It will largely replace interpersonal networking.**

REALITY: The two forms of networking are not mutually exclusive; they complement each other. Indeed, a great deal of hype currently surrounds the self-proclaimed "job search revolution" which primarily involves the application of computer technology to the recruitment and job search processes. The danger of this revolution is to overestimate its effectiveness in the job search process and thereby give job seekers the false impression that jobs can best be found on the Internet or through various electronic job banks and on-line career services.

It may dissuade many job seekers from using more effective interpersonal networking techniques. So far electronic networking primarily involves moving classified ads from print media to electronic media and allowing employers to cut recruitment costs by searching for candidates on-line or through electronic job banks—inexpensive alternatives to placing classified ads and using executive search firms. Most of these networks are shaped and controlled by employers because they are the ones who directly pay for the operation of the electronic networks. So far employers disproportionately use such services for recruiting individuals with high-tech skills. While electronic networking will increasingly play an important role in the employment process, it is no substitute for interpersonal networking. The central problem remains communication between employers and job seekers. Electronic networking can result in useful information and contacts, interpersonal networking best resolves this communication problem. Thus, you are well advised to conduct both interpersonal and electronic networking, but spend most of your time perfecting your interpersonal networking skills.

RESUMES AND NETWORKING

MYTH 10:   **One should network rather than use resumes and letters for finding a job.**

REALITY: Networking is no substitute for the more traditional means of communicating your qualifications to employers—resumes and letters. Again, confusion often arises over the purpose and role of both resumes and networking in the job search. During certain stages of one's job search, resumes and letters must be written and disseminated. This occurs after identifying one's motivated abilities and setting an objective. Resumes may be used to help uncover job leads, and networking helps identify to whom to send resumes and letters. At the same time, resumes and letters play an important role in the networking process. The resume, for example, should be presented at the very end of an informational interview for the purpose of receiving advice on how to improve its content as well as for summarizing your goals, experience, and qualifications. You will want your networking contact to **refer you and your resume to others** who might be interested in your job search and qualifications. At the same time, you must write different types of letters as part of your networking campaign. To conduct a job search or engage in networking activities without a powerful one or two-page resume, or without using referral and thank-you letters, is simply foolish. Always keep copies of your resume close to you. You never know when you will use it as part of your networking activities.

RESUMES AND INFORMATIONAL INTERVIEWS

MYTH 11:   **I should send a resume with my approach letter when initiating a networking contact.**

REALITY: Never, never, never send a resume to a contact unless the individual requests it. Remember, the purpose of networking is to get information, advice, and referrals relevant to uncovering job leads and interviews. The resume should only be revealed at the end of the informational interview—for a critique.

INFORMATIONAL INTERVIEWS

MYTH 12:   **In the informational interview you want to impress upon the interviewer that you are qualified for a job.**

REALITY: The informational interview is an important means of (1) exchanging information about job alternatives relevant to your interests, experience, and qualifications; (2) learning how to strengthen your job search; and (3) receive referrals for expanding your networks. In an informational interview, you are the interviewer and the other person is the interviewee. Interviewers need not impress their qualifications on interviewees unless they are confused as to whom is conducting the interview and for what purpose.

REJECTIONS

MYTH 13:   **You will seldom be rejected for an informational interview.**

REALITY: This is true if you approach the informational interview properly. However, if you (1) only focus on persons who have the power to hire, and (2) attempt to use the informational interview to get job interviews and offers, you may experience many rejections. Few people are interested in assisting others who primarily want to use them for personal gain.

INITIATING CONTACTS

MYTH 14:   **The best way to initiate contacts for networking is to write a letter requesting an informational interview.**

REALITY: While letters play an important role in a job search if written and used properly, a telephone call is likely to be more effective because you will receive immediate feedback and you will be initially screened for the informational interview.

REFERRALS

MYTH 15:   **It is always best to use referrals in the networking process.**

REALITY: Referrals are important in making contacts, but they are not necessarily the best way to proceed. Referrals help ease the process of introducing oneself to strangers, and they build on relationships of others. However, too much emphasis is often placed on referrals to the detriment of taking individual initiative in establishing cold contacts. Indeed, you may do just as well on your own by making contacts with strangers. The problem with referrals is twofold: (1) they are often time consuming because they rely too much on personal relationships, and (2) you cannot be certain of the nature of the relationship between the sources of your referral and your networking contact, i.e., whether it is positive or negative for you. Cold calling techniques can be more effective because they can be initiated rapidly and they do not involve a questionable third party relationship. However, for shy individuals who have difficulty making cold contacts, the referral method will be the easier and you will receive few rejections.

LONG-DISTANCE NETWORKING

MYTH 16:   **Networking does not work well when you attempt to conduct a job search in an unfamiliar community. In such cases it is best to respond to vacancy announcements, contact employment agencies, or send resumes and letters directly to prospective employers.**

REALITY: Networking is not limited to the community in which you live. It can work anywhere, if you know what you are doing and can develop an effective long-distance job search campaign. If you are targeting your job search on another community, it is best to develop both individual and organizational contacts by telephone and personal visits to the community. While you may have to rely more on cold calling techniques, the techniques should work well if you spend the proper amount of time using them to uncover informational interviewing leads.

COOPERATION

MYTH 17:   **Most people are reluctant to share information about their job or career.**

REALITY: Most people, regardless of their position or status, love to talk about their work and give advice to both friends and strangers. You can learn the most about job opportunities and alternative careers by talking to such people through your networking activities.

APPROACHING STRANGERS

MYTH 18:   **I'm too shy to approach strangers through either referrals or cold calls. I'm just not assertive enough. I'm especially afraid of being rejected.**

REALITY: You need not be overly assertive in the process of networking. There are many effective techniques that can help overcome shyness. Best of all, the process of networking is aimed at sharing information—something that does not require assertiveness nor involve stress commonly associated with shyness. Since you are not asking for a job and thus not putting others in an uncomfortable position of considering you for a job, you will encounter few rejections in the process of net-working.

PLANNING AND LUCK

MYTH 19:   **You can plan all you want, but getting a job is really a function of good luck.**

REALITY: Luck is more than just chance. Above all, luck in the job search is a function of being in the right place at the right time to take advantage of opportunities that come your way. Therefore, the best way to have luck come your way is to **plan to be in many different places at many different times**. You can do this by putting together an excellent resume and network with it in both the advertised and hidden job markets. If you are persistent in implementing your plans, luck may strike you many times!

ADDITIONAL REALITIES

You will encounter several other realities in the process of developing your networks and networking for information, advice, and referrals. Among these are the following:

REALITY: **You will find less competition for high-level jobs than for middle and low-level jobs.**

Hiring procedures for middle and low-level jobs tend to be more formalized, requiring resumes and application forms, because of the high competition for these jobs. As a result, networking may be less effective for these levels of employment. Competition is generally less keen for higher-level positions where hiring procedures are less formalized. It is at this level where networking may be more effective.

REALITY: **Your networks and networking activities might include individuals in personnel offices, but don't expect them to be in control of hiring decisions.**

Personnel offices primarily screen candidates for employers who are found in operating units of organizations. Knowing this, you should expand your job search efforts toward those who are more directly involved in the actual hiring process.

REALITY: **Politics are both ubiquitous and dangerous in many organizations.**

If you think you are above politics, you may quickly become one of its victims. Unfortunately, you only learn about "local politics" **after** you accept a position and begin relating to the different players in the organization. It is wise to learn about the internal politics of an organization prior to accepting a position. You can do this most effectively through your networking activities.

REALITY: **It is best to narrow in or "rifle" your job search on particular organizations and individuals rather than broaden or "shotgun" it to many alternatives.**

Your networking activities increasingly require you to conduct a well organized and focused job search. While initially you may not have a clear idea of what you want to do and where you hope to do it, the more you network and conduct informational interviews, the more you should become focused on specific career goals and organizations. If you fail to focus your job search, you will most likely present a confused image to your network contacts as well as to potential employers.

REALITY: **Employment firms, personnel agencies, and online career services may not be helpful in your job search.**

Most employment firms, personnel agencies, and online career services work for employers and themselves rather than for applicants. Few have your best interests at heart. Use them only after you have investigated their effectiveness. Avoid firms that require up-front money for a promise of performance. In the end your best friend in finding a job will be **you** and your own well organized job search centered around networking activities.

REALITY: **Most people can make satisfying job and career changes.**

If you minimize efforts in the advertised job market and concentrate instead on planning and implementing a well organized job search tailored to the realities of the hidden job market, you should be successful in making a job or career change that is most compatible with your interests, skills, and experience.

REALITY: **"Connections" or "pull" can be very effective in finding a job or changing careers.**

Many employers welcome informal contacts with candidates who are connected to friends, relatives, and acquaintances. Such connections perform an important function within the job market: they provide basic screening of individuals by those who know the candidate. Such screening is preferable to much of the screening information acquired from the formal hiring process—letters of recommendations, interviews, and conversations with former employers. A personal contact, acquired through networking, often provides more reliable and trusted information about candidates than information received from strangers who frequently have a vested interest in accenting the positives rather than revealing the negatives of former employees.

PREPARE FOR ADVICE AND CHAOS

As you conduct your job search and networking activities, you will encounter many of these and other myths and realities about how you should relate to the job market. Several people will give you advice. While much of this advice will be useful, a great deal of it will be useless and misleading. You should be skeptical of well-meaning individuals who most likely will reiterate the same job and career myths. You should be particularly leery of those who try to **sell** you their advice.

Always remember you are entering a relatively disorganized and chaotic job market which has the appearance of organization and coherence. If you approach this job market properly, you will encounter numerous and exciting job opportunities. Your task is to organize the chaos around your skills and interests. You must convince prospective employers that they will like you more than other "qualified" candidates. Networking should play a key role in organizing the job market and communicating your qualifications to employers.

5

IDENTIFYING AND BUILDING YOUR NETWORKS

Your network may be your most prized yet neglected resource for finding a job or changing careers. *"Who you know"* and *"who knows you"* are likely to be just as important to finding a job as *"What you can do."* You must first identify who defines your current network before you can develop, expand, and use networks in the job search process through the use of prospecting, networking, and informational interviewing techniques.

IDENTIFY YOUR NETWORK MEMBERS

Everyone has a network whether they realize it or not. It consists of individuals they know and interact with and who influence each other's behavior. Perhaps you regularly meet with 10 people on a daily basis. These individuals may constitute the most important **members** in your network: spouse, children, neighbors, boss, fellow workers, professional colleagues, friends, and acquaintances. You **know** their characteristics, how they behave, and to what degree they relate to you. You have **expectations** concerning how these individuals will behave toward you, and they have expectations about how you will relate to them. You **play different roles** depending on whom you interact with. During much of the day you may play the roles of employee, supervisor, and professional colleague, but during other times of the day you perform the roles of spouse, parent, friend, neighbor, and/or customer.

At the same time, individuals defining your network also have expectations that influence your own behavior. Your work habits, for example, may include arriving at work five minutes early each day. You do this because your supervisor expects you to be punctual, and you believe it's important to impress upon both your supervisor and co-workers the importance of punctuality. Individuals in your network know you as someone who usually plays a specific role vis-a-vis them-selves: spouse, father, supervisor, colleague, friend, or acquaintance. Seldom do you present yourself to the same individual in more than one role.

You know many other individuals whom you may or may not interact with on a regular basis. For example, you have relatives that you may see only once a year; an old high school friend you still exchange Christmas cards with; a sorority sister you haven't seen in over seven years; a former high school or college teacher; or your doctor, lawyer, banker, insurance agent, and minister whom you only occasionally meet. While not as important to you on a daily basis, many of these individuals may play critical roles during certain times of your life. All should be included in your network.

DEVELOP A CONTACT LIST

One of the best ways to identify members in your network is to develop a contact list. Begin by making a list of 200 people you know. This list will most likely include relatives, neighbors, fellow workers, former employers, alumni, friends, acquaintances, bankers, doctors, lawyers, ministers, and professional colleagues. Perhaps only 10 of these people will be in your immediate day-to-day network. The others may be former friends, acquaintances, or your Aunt Betsy you haven't seen in over 10 years. If you have difficulty developing such a list, refresh your memory by referring to the following checklist of categories:

CATEGORIES FOR CONTACT LIST

___ Friends (consult your Christmas card list)

___ Neighbors (past and present)

___ Social acquaintances (group and club members)

___ Classmates (high school and college)

___ Local alumni

___ People you consulted or wrote a check to during the past 12 months:

    ___ tradespeople, drugstore owner
    ___ doctor, dentist, optician, therapist
    ___ lawyer, accountant, real estate agent
    ___ insurance agent, stock broker, travel agent

___ Local bank manager

___ Relatives (immediate and distant)

___ Politicians (local, state, and national)

___ Chamber of Commerce members

___ Pastors, ministers

___ Church members

___ Trade association members

___ Professional organization executives

___ Other members of professional organizations

___ People you meet at conferences or conventions

___ Speakers at meetings you've attended

___ Business club executives and members (Rotary, Kiwanis, Jaycees, etc.)

___ Representatives of direct-sales businesses (real estate, insurance, Amway, Shaklee, Avon)

___ Other

After developing your comprehensive list of contacts, classify the names into four different categories:

- Those in influential positions or who have hiring authority.

- Those with job leads.

- Those most likely to refer you to others.

- Those with long-distance contacts.

Select at least 25 individuals from your list of 200 names for initiating your first round of contacts. You are now ready to begin an active prospecting and networking campaign which will enable you to expand your present network considerably by linking it to others' networks. This campaign should lead to informational interviews, formal job interviews, and job offers.

EXPAND YOUR NETWORK

Methods for expanding one's networks are closely related to several face-to-face sales techniques used in the insurance, real estate, and other direct-sales businesses: prospecting, pyramiding, and client referral systems. In the job search the analogous techniques become **prospecting**, **networking**, and **informational interviewing**. Your job search goals and situations will be similar to those found in many successful businesses:

- Your goal is to sell an important high quality product—yourself—by shopping around for a good buyer—an employer.

- The buyer wants to be assured, based upon previous and current demonstration, that he or she is investing in a high quality and reliable product.

- Face-to-face communication, rather than impersonal advertising, remains the best way to make buying/selling decisions.

- When the buyer and seller exchange information on each other, the quality of information improves and the new relationship will probably be mutually beneficial, and satisfying.

The job search techniques of prospecting, networking, and informational interviewing are relatively easy to learn and use. However, you must first understand the nature of networks, pyramids, and referral systems used in sales. As noted earlier, a network consists of you and people you know, who are important to you, and with whom you interact most frequently. Many of these people influence your behavior. Others may also influence your behavior but you interact with them less frequently. As illustrated earlier on page 38, your network may consist of family, friends, assisters, professional colleagues, fellow workers, and your supervisor. Your network of relationships involves **people**—not data, things, or knowledge of a particular subject area—who may provide you with the most critical assistance in your job search—information, advice, and referrals.

BUILD YOUR NETWORKS
THROUGH PROSPECTING

The key to successful networking is an active and routine **prospecting campaign**. Salespersons in insurance, real estate, Amway, Shaklee, and other direct-sales businesses understand the importance and principles of prospecting; indeed, many have turned the art of prospecting into a science!

Prospecting is conducted by means of letters, telephone calls, faxes, and face-to-face meetings. The quickest way to generate numerous prospects is to use the **telephone**. The degree of effectiveness, however, depends on whether you initiate the call based on a referral or make a cold call. The cold call is the least effective prospecting method, but it is very efficient and thus generates a much larger volume of contacts than any other prospecting method. **Letters** require follow-up—preferably by telephone—to be effective. While **face-to-face meetings** will be your most effective prospecting method, such meetings are very time consuming; they will cut down on the overall efficiency of your prospecting campaign.

The key to successful networking is an active and routine prospecting campaign which operates according to the principle of probability.

The basic operating principle behind prospecting techniques is **probability**: the number of sales you make is a direct function of the amount of effort you put into developing new contacts and following-through. Expect no more than a 10 percent acceptance rate: for every ten people you contact, nine will reject you and one will accept you. Therefore, the more people you contact, the more acceptances you will receive. If you want to be successful, you must collect many more "nos" than "yeses." In a 10 percent probability situation, you need to contact 100 people for 10 successes.

These prospecting principles are extremely useful for your job search. Like sales situations, the job search is a highly ego-involved activity often characterized by numerous rejections accompanied by a few acceptances. While no one wants to be rejected, few people are willing and able to handle more than a few rejections. They take a "no" as a sign of personal failure—and quit prematurely. If they persisted longer, they would achieve success after a few more "nos." Furthermore, if their prospecting activities were focused on **gathering information** rather than making sales, they would considerably minimize the number of rejections they receive.

Knowing these probabilistic negative and positive outcomes of most prospecting campaigns, your best approach to prospecting in a job search is to:

- **Prospect** for job leads.

- **Accept rejections** as part of the game.

- **Link prospecting** to networking and informational interviewing.

- **Keep prospecting** for more "yeses," contacts, information, advice, and referrals that will eventually translate into job interviews and offers.

Prospecting involves contacting people in your network and building new networks for information and job leads. Many people in direct-sales quit at this point because they lack the prerequisites for success— patience, perseverance, and a positive attitude. Prospecting techniques require you to:

- Develop enthusiastic one-on-one appointments and informational interview presentations.

- Be consistent and persistent in how you present your case.

- Give prospecting and follow-up high priorities in your overall daily routine.

- Believe you will be successful given your persistence with these techniques; prospecting is a probability game involving both successes and failures.

MAKE MANY CONTACTS

A good prospecting pace to begin with is to make two new contacts each day. Start by contacting people in your immediate network. Let them know you are conducting a job search, but emphasize that you are only doing research. Ask for a few moments of their time to discuss your information needs. You are only seeking **information and advice** at this time—not a job.

Prospecting and networking, above all, requires **persistence**. For example, it takes about 20 minutes to initiate a contact by telephone—longer by letter. If you contact at least one person in your immediate circle of contacts each day, your prospecting should yield 15 new contacts each week for a total investment of less than two hours. Each of these new contacts could possibly yield three additional contacts or 45 new referrals. However, some contacts will yield more than three and others may yield none. If you develop contacts in this manner, you will create a series of small pyramids or networks, as illustrated on page 83. If you expand your prospecting from one to three new contacts each day, you could generate 135 new contacts and referrals in a single week. If you continue this same level of activity over a two-month period, it is possible to create over 1,000 new contacts and referrals! At this pace, your odds of uncovering job opportunities, being invited to formal job interviews, and receiving job offers will increase dramatically.

The more contacts you make, the more useful information, advice, and job leads you will receive. If your job search bogs down, you probably need to increase your prospecting activities. Indeed, the single most important reason for slow and ineffective job searches that result in complaints that *"there are no jobs out there for me"* is the failure to conduct an active and persistent prospecting campaign that leads to referrals and informational interviews.

The linkages and pyramids on page 83 constitute your **job search network**. Always remember to nurture and manage this network so it performs well in generating information and job leads. As you follow-through on making new contacts, expect about half to result in referrals. However, a few of your contacts will continue to give you referrals beyond the initial ones. Consequently, **you need to continually develop new contacts while maintaining communication with prior contacts**. When conducting informational interviews, as we will see shortly, ask your contacts to keep you in mind if they hear of anyone who might be interested in your qualifications.

While prospecting is an excellent way to create contacts, it also helps you develop a realistic objective, effective interview skills, and self-confidence. In using this system, you will seldom be turned down for an informational interview. You should uncover vacancies on the hidden job market as well as place yourself in a positive position to take advantage of such opportunities.

DEVELOPING NETWORKS THROUGH DAILY PROSPECTING

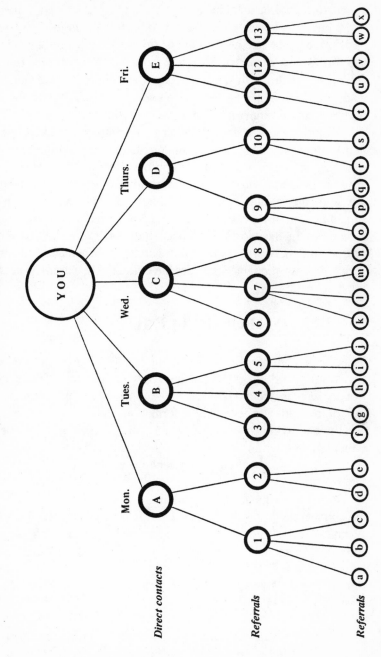

Never directly ask for a job while prospecting, networking, and conducting informational interviews. Asking for a job puts your contact under pressure; it is the quickest way to be politely shown the door. The basic principle behind networking is: **the best way to get a job is never ask for a job directly; always ask for information, advice, and referrals**. By doing this, you will be interviewed, your resume will be read, and if you listen to the advice you receive, you eventually will be offered a job through one or more of your contacts.

Our prospecting system is similar to the networking techniques used in the direct-sales businesses. These proven, low-keyed sales techniques require persistence, a personable approach to people, and the ability to share a "product" and offer an opportunity to prospective buyers. This low stress approach does not threaten individuals by asking them to buy something, or, in your case, give you a job. Some of the most successful businesses in the world have been built on this simple one-on-one prospecting, networking and referral strategy. When adapted to the job search process, the same strategies have resulted in extremely successful job placements.

TELEPHONE FOR JOB LEADS

Telephone communication plays an important role in prospecting, networking, and informational interviewing activities. However, controversy centers around how and when to use the telephone in prospecting for job leads and generating informational interviewing. Some people recommend writing a letter and waiting for a written or telephone reply. Others suggest writing a letter and following it with a telephone call. Still others argue you should use the telephone exclusively rather than write letters.

How you use the telephone will indicate what type of job search you are conducting. Exclusive reliance on the telephone is a technique used by highly formalized job clubs which operate phone banks for generating job leads. Using the Yellow Pages as the guide to employers, a job club member may call as many as 50 employers a day to schedule interviews. A rather aggressive yet typical telephone dialogue goes something like this:

"Hello, my name is Jim Baker. I would like to speak to the head of the training department. By the way, what is the name of the training director?"

"You want to talk to Ms. Stevens. Her number is 723-8191, or do you want me to connect you?"

"Hello, Ms. Stevens. This is Jim Baker. I have several years of training experience as both a trainer and developer of training materials. I would like to meet with you to discuss possible openings in your department for someone with my qualifications. Would it be possible to see you on Friday at 2pm?"

Not surprising, this telephone approach generates many *"nos."* If you have a hard time handling rejections, this telephone approach will help you confront your anxieties. The principle behind this approach is **probability**: for every 25 telephone *"nos"* you receive, you will probably get one or two *"yeses."* Success is just 25 telephone calls away! If you start calling prospective employers at 9am and finish your 12 calls by noon, you should generate at least one or two interviews. That's not bad for three hours of job search work. It beats sending out letters.

The telephone is more efficient than writing letters. However, its effectiveness is questionable.

The telephone is more efficient than writing letters. However, its effectiveness is questionable. When you use the telephone in this manner, you are basically asking for a job. You are asking the employer: *"Do you have a job for me?"* There is nothing subtle or particularly professional about this approach. It is effective in uncovering particular types of job leads for particular types of individuals. If you need any job in a hurry, this is one of the most efficient ways of finding employment. It's much better than standing in line at the state employment office! But if you are more concerned with finding a job that is right for you—a job you do well and enjoy doing, one that is fit for you—this telephone approach may be inappropriate.

You must use your own judgment in determining when and how to use the telephone for prospecting and networking purposes. As we've outlined elsewhere (***Dynamite Tele-Search***, Impact, 1995), there are appropriate times and methods for using the telephone, and these should relate to your job search goals and needs. For example, you must be prepared to handle a formidable gatekeeper in today's telephone communication—voice mail. You'll also need to develop appealing telephone scripts that generate positive responses to your telephone inquiries and increase your overall networking effectiveness. We'll review these techniques with sample telephone dialogues in Chapter 6.

For most job seekers, the more conventional approach of writing a letter followed by a telephone call can work well in building networks. While you take the initiative in scheduling an appointment, you do not put the individual on the spot by asking for a job. You are only seeking information, advice, and referrals. This low-keyed approach results in numerous acceptances and has a higher probability of paying off with interviews than the aggressive telephone request. You should be trying to uncover jobs that are right for you rather than any job that happens to pop up from a telephoning blitz.

The key to networking success is to focus on gathering information while also learning to handle rejections.

MINIMIZE REJECTIONS

These prospecting and networking methods are effective. While they are responsible for building, maintaining, and expanding multi-million dollar businesses, they work extremely well for job hunters. But they only work if you are patient and persist. The key to networking success is to focus on gathering information while also learning to handle rejections. Learn from rejections, forget them, and go on to more productive networking activities. The major reason direct-sales people fail is because they don't persist. The reason they don't persist is because they either can't take, or get tired of taking, rejections.

Rejections are no fun, especially in such an ego-involved activity as a job search. But you will encounter rejections as you travel on the road toward job search success. This road is strewn with individuals who quit prematurely because they were rejected four or five times. Don't be one of them!

Our prospecting and networking techniques differ from sales approaches in one major respect: we have special techniques for minimizing the number of rejections. If handled properly, at least 50 percent—maybe as many as 90 percent—of your prospects will turn into *"yeses"* rather than *"nos."* The reason for this unusually high acceptance rate is how you introduce and handle yourself before your prospects. Many insurance agents and direct distributors expect a 90 percent rejection rate, because they are trying to sell specific products potential clients may or may not need. Most people don't like to be put on the spot—especially when it is in their own home or office—to make a decision to buy a product.

BE HONEST AND SINCERE

The principles of selling yourself in the job market are similar. People don't want to be put on the spot. They feel uncomfortable if they think you expect them to give you a job. Thus, you should never introduce yourself to a prospect by asking them for a job or a job lead. You should do just the opposite: relieve their anxiety by mentioning that you are not looking for a job from them—only job information and advice. You must be honest and sincere in communicating these intentions to your contact. The biggest turn-off for individuals targeted for informational interviews is insincere job seekers who try to use this as a mechanism to get a job.

Your approach to prospects must be subtle, honest, and professional. You are seeking information, advice, and referrals in several areas:

- Job opportunities

- Your job search approach

- Your resume

- Others who may have similar information, advice, and referrals.

Most people willingly volunteer such information. They generally like to talk about themselves, their careers, and others. They like to give advice. This approach flatters individuals by placing them in the role of the expert-advisor. Who doesn't want to be recognized as an expert-advisor, especially on such a critical topic as one's employment?

This approach should yield a great deal of information, advice, and referrals from your prospects. One other important outcome should result form using this approach: people will **remember** you as the person who made them feel at ease and who received their valuable advice. If they hear of job opportunities for someone with your qualifications, chances are they will contact you with the information. After contacting 100 prospects, you will have created 100 sets of eyes and ears to help you in your job search!

OBSERVE THE 5R's OF INFORMATIONAL INTERVIEWING

When you engage your prospects in the informational interviewing process, you want them to engage in the 5R's of informational interviewing:

- **Reveal** useful information and advice.

- **Refer** you to others for additional information and advice.

- **Read** and **revise** your resume.

- **Remember** you for future reference.

If you follow these principles, you should join the ranks of thousands of successful job seekers who paid a great deal of money learning these same principles from highly-paid professionals. Save your money by **implementing** the principles outlined here.

6

DEVELOPING JOB LEADS AND GETTING JOB INTERVIEWS

While prospecting is the most important technique for expanding your networks, the informational interview is the major networking method used for conducting an effective job search. Again, your goal is to get information, advice, and referrals that may turn into job leads and interviews. You do this by developing a very effective informational interviewing approach to individuals in your expanded network.

UNDERSTAND THE EMPLOYER'S PROBLEM AND PERSPECTIVE

Put yourself in the position of an employer again for a moment. Your problem is how to go about filling a job vacancy. If you advertise the position, you may be bombarded with hundreds of applications, phone calls, and walk-ins. While you do want to hire the best qualified individual for the job, you simply don't have the time nor patience to review scores of applications. Even if you use a P.O. Box number, the paperwork may be overwhelming. Furthermore, with limited information from application forms, cover letters, and resumes, you find it hard to identify the best qualified individuals to invite for an interview; indeed, many candidates look the same on paper!

So what do you do? How can you best cut through this process? You might hire a professional job search firm to take on all of this additional work. On the other hand, you may want to better control the hiring process. Like many other employers, you begin by calling your friends, acquaintances, and other business associates and ask if they or someone else might know of any good candidates for the position. If they can't help, you ask them to give you a call should they learn of anyone qualified for your vacancy. You, in effect, create your own hidden job market—an informal information network for locating desirable candidates. Your trusted contacts initially screen the candidates in the process of referring them to you.

CONDUCT INFORMATIONAL INTERVIEWS

Based on this understanding of the employer's perspective, what should you do to best improve your chances of getting an interview and job offer? Remember, the employer needs to solve a personnel problem. By **networking** and **conducting informational interviews**, you help the employer solve his or her problem by giving them a chance to examine what you can offer them. You gain several advantages by conducting these interviews:

- You are less likely to encounter rejections since you are not asking for a job—only information, advice, referrals, and to be remembered.

- You go after higher level positions.

- You encounter little competition.

- You go directly to the people who have influence in the hiring process.

- You are likely to be invited to job interviews based upon the referrals you receive.

This job search approach has a much higher probability of generating job interviews and offers than the more traditional shot-gunning and advertised job market approaches.

While you will encounter some *"nos"* in your search for *"yeses,"* informational interviews minimize the number of *"nos"* you will collect. Using this approach, you seldom will be turned down for an interview. In fact, most people will be happy to share their experiences with you and give you information, advice, and referrals. Most important, informational interviews help you overcome the likelihood of rejection.

The first rule in conducting informational interviews is to never ask for a job.

The first rule in conducting informational interviews is to never ask for a job. When you ask for a job, or ask to be interviewed for a job (which you do when you send off your resume), you set yourself up to receive a rejection. If no job is available, you put the employer in an uncomfortable position of telling you *"no."* If you apply for an advertised opening, you will probably get lost in the herd of applicants. On the other hand, if you request an interview for information and advice—not a job—you are likely to get a *"yes."*

Informational interviews will help you build networks for locating the better jobs and careers. For example, look at the classifieds in your local newspaper. Most of the positions listed are either lower level positions or they require a high level of technical skills—in other words, positions that are difficult to fill. Since the jobs you learn about through your networks are often neither advertised nor competitive, your odds of getting a good job improve considerably. As you continue making new contacts through additional referrals, you will build a large network of job contacts. Individuals in your network will be your eyes and ears for locating job opportunities that are appropriate to your goals and skills.

ENTER THE BACK DOOR

Regardless of what you have heard about affirmative action, equal opportunity, the need to advertise positions, classified ads, and online job postings, the unadvertised or hidden job market still exists and continues to thrive. It is not our intent to sit in judgment of what should or should not be proper employment behavior. Rather, our job is to help you understand the realities of today's job market and prepare you to handle these realities to your maximum advantage.

Suffice it to say that you can gain access to most jobs through both a front door and a back door. Long lines normally form at the front door. If you conduct informational interviews and network, you should be able to enter through the back door. Job seekers find this entrance infinitely more responsive and rewarding than standing in line. You, too, may wish to join the successful job seekers who know how to get through the door to see the person who has the power to hire.

You can gain access to most jobs through both a front door and a back door. You'll find the back door to be most effective.

Your information/networking interviews help you by-pass personnel offices and other gatekeepers who lack the power to hire. Personnel offices have many functions, but they seldom hire. They advertise positions, take applications, administer tests, and many conduct initial screening interviews. The hiring function usually rests with the department head/manager for mid-level positions; upper management hires for senior upper-level positions. One of your initial job search tasks should be to identify who makes the hiring decision in the organizations for which you seek employment. Once you have this information, you'll be in a better position to effectively target your networking activities.

APPROACH THE RIGHT PEOPLE

Whom should you contact within an organization for an informational interview? It is difficult to give one best answer to this question. Ideally you should contact people who are busy, who have the power to hire, and who are knowledgeable about the organization. The least likely candidate will be someone in the personnel department. Most often the heads of operating units are the most busy, powerful, and knowledgeable individuals in the organization. However, getting access to such individuals may be difficult. At the same time, some people at the top may appear to be informed and powerful, but they may lack information on the day-to-day personnel changes or their influence is limited in the hiring process.

Aim for the busy, powerful, and informed, but be prepared to settle for less.

We recommend contacting a variety of people. Aim for the busy, powerful, and informed, but be prepared to settle for less. Secretaries, receptionists, and the person you want to meet may refer you to others. From a practical standpoint, you may have to take whomever you can schedule an appointment with. Sometimes people who are not busy can be helpful. Talk to a secretary or receptionist sometime about working in the organization. You may be surprised with what you learn!

Nonetheless, you will conduct informational interviews with different types of people. Some will be friends, relatives, or acquaintances. Others will be referrals or new contacts. You will gain the easiest access to people you already know. This can usually be done informally by telephone. You might meet at their home or office or at a restaurant.

USE THE TELEPHONE
FREQUENTLY AND EFFECTIVELY

Don't expect to conduct all of your informational interviews in person. To do so is expecting too much from busy people and may be naive given the busy nature of communication these days. Be prepared to conduct many networking activities over the telephone rather than in face-to-face settings. It is both to your advantage and others to do so. Busy people often prefer using the telephone to scheduling meetings. The quality of information you receive over the telephone may even be better than in face-to-face meetings since telephone conversations are less inhibited than those taking place in face-to-face settings. In fact, nearly 80 percent of all your networking activities can be conveniently conducted over the telephone.

Nearly 80 percent of all your networking activities can be conveniently conducted over the telephone.

Effective telephone communication is easier said than done. Many people, for example, are reluctant to pick up the telephone to initiate contacts with strangers. They feel uncomfortable and awkward, afraid they will say the wrong things or make fools of themselves. This should not happen to you since you may quickly find that your telephone is your best networking friend.

Telephone networking should play a central role in your job search. The telephone is an extremely efficient way to quickly acquire useful information, make job contacts, and schedule job interviews. A few simple telephone techniques should put you on the right road to becoming a effective telephone networker. Here are few examples of how you can initiate both cold calls and referral interviews over the telephone:

Cold Call for Contact Information

CALLER: *"Hi. This is Terri Bays. I'm trying to contact the person in charge of marketing. Who would that be?"*

RECEIVER: *"That's Eric Walton. He's the Director."*

CALLER: *"I need to contact him about some marketing concerns. Does he have a direct number or an extension number?"*

RECEIVER: *"His number is 281-7821. Should I transfer you?"*

ANALYSIS: This is a straightforward call for information. It follows the basic *"I'm X, who's Y, and how do I reach Y?"* format. Most gatekeepers volunteer this information with no questions asked—if you mention that you have "business" to conduct.

Cold Call With Message

CALLER: *"This is Terri Bays calling for Eric Walton."*

RECEIVER: *"Mr. Walton is in a meeting at present. Would you like to leave a message?"*

CALLER: *"Yes. Could you tell him Terri Bays called. My number is 731-3000. I would like to speak with him concerning his work in . . . . I'll be in my office the rest of the day as well as between 9:00am and 4:00pm tomorrow. Thank you."*

ANALYSIS: The caller immediately identifies herself and requests to speak with the person. Given this direct *"I'm X calling for Y"* approach, the gatekeeper may assume you know the person and thus be more willing to field your call. When making such a cold call, you should leave a complete message in which you (1) state your name, (2) leave your phone number, (3) indicate the nature of your business, and (4) identify your availability during the next 24 hours for a return call. Whether or not you receive a return call depends in part on the quality of your message concerning the nature of your business. Leave enough information that will motivate the person to return your call—not too much nor too little. The same message should be left if the person is immediately reached by voice mail or the gatekeeper puts you through to a voice mailbox.

Cold Call Screened By Gatekeeper

CALLER: *"This is Terri Bays calling for Eric Walton."*

RECEIVER: *"Where are you calling from and what is the nature of your business?"*

CALLER: *"I'm calling from Indianapolis. I would like to speak with Mr. Walton about his work in . . ."*

RECEIVER: *"Let me check to see if he is available."*

Cold Call Making Direct Contact

CALLER: *"This is Terri Bays calling for Eric Walton."*

RECEIVER: *"Speaking."*

CALLER: *"I'm calling about your work in marketing. I'm in the process of gathering information on opportunities in international marketing and thought you could be a good person to talk with because of your extensive experience with Bellows International. Do you have a few minutes or would it be better if I called back at a more convenient time?"*

RECEIVER: *"I'm really not sure I can be of much help. I'm very busy right now. What type of information do you need?"*

CALLER: *"I recently completed my Bachelor's Degree in International Marketing at Indiana University. I speak Russian and have traveled extensively throughout Eastern Europe. I really want to start my career in this fascinating part of the world, but I'm not sure how to best proceed at this point. I'm now gathering information on pharmaceutical companies that have begun marketing their products in Russia and the Newly Independent States. Since I know you've done extensive international marketing, do you know who the major players are in this region? I'm trying to identify four or five of the key companies that are either currently in the area or interested in expanding their operations there."*

ANALYSIS: The caller has a nice low-keyed approach that is considerate, pleasant, and persistent. She immediately establishes common ground by linking her background to the receiver's experience. While seeking information and contacts, she clearly communicates her interest and enthusiasm by mentioning her educational background and travel experience. She invites the receiver to give her advice and thus creates the role of counselor for the receiver. She is not asking for a job—only information and advice. She'll most likely ask for referrals at the very end of this conversation. Best of all for a cold call, she sounds interesting, intelligent, and adventuresome. This is someone the receiver will probably decide to talk with for more than just a few minutes. Even though she is a stranger, he will probably like her and want to help her.

Referral With Gatekeeper

CALLER: *"Hi, this is Jim Taylor calling for Margaret Davis."*

RECEIVER: *"Miss Davis is in a meeting at present. Would you like to leave a message?"*

CALLER: *"Yes. Could you tell her Jim Taylor called. My number is 214-2790. Melissa Warner recommended that I call her about her work in . . . . I'll be in my office the rest of the day as well as between 9:00am and 4:00pm tomorrow. Thank you."*

ANALYSIS: Similar to the Terri Bays/Eric Walton cold call, the caller in this case immediately identifies himself and requests to speak with the person—the direct *"I'm X calling for Y"* approach. The gatekeeper will probably assume the caller knows the person. When the caller learns the person is not available, he leaves a message mentioning his referral contact. He has a high probability of getting a return call. He should leave the same message if he immediately encounters voice mail or the gatekeeper puts him through to a voice mailbox.

Referral Direct

CALLER: *"This is Terri Bays calling for Eric Walton."*

RECEIVER: *"Speaking."*

CALLER: *"John Pinkerton recommended that I call about your work in marketing."*

RECEIVER: *"How is John? I haven't spoken with him for some time."*

CALLER: *"John's doing great. He just returned from a two-month research project in the Ukraine. He's doing some fascinating work on a pilot agricultural marketing project sponsored by the UN. In fact, he recommended that I call you because you taught together in the Marketing Department at Michigan State University several years ago. He spoke very highly of you."*

RECEIVER: *"That's great to hear. John's always doing interesting and innovative work. Please give him my regards. So, how can I help you?"*

CALLER: *"I recently completed my Bachelor's Degree in International Marketing at Indiana University. I speak Russian and have traveled extensively . . . "*

ANALYSIS: This is the most effective type of call you can make. It helps you quickly develop and expand your job search network. The caller already has a personal contact for establishing common ground. In contrast to other types of calls, referral calls often begin with a few moments of small talk. This type of small talk helps transfer the personal relationship existing between your referral and the receiver to you. It helps develop a cooperative relationship that should result in greater depth of information, advice, and referrals.

You need to make several types of follow-up calls throughout your job search. Failure to follow-up is one of the major reasons many job seekers have difficulty making progress in the job market. You simply must follow-up often and do so by telephone. The following are the most frequent type of follow-up calls you need to make.

Thank You Follow-Up

CALLER: *"Hi, this is Jerry Winton calling for Jonathan Arthur."*

RECEIVER: *"Speaking."*

CALLER: *"Thanks so much for referring me to Jill Balinger last week. You were right. She really knows the leasing business, and I'm most impressed with the work she is doing in marine leasing. We had a wonderful talk this morning and she invited me to meet with her next Tuesday about a position with her firm. I just wanted to let you know how much I appreciated your advice and reference. I'll let you know the outcome."*

ANALYSIS: Not only is such a thank you call a thoughtful thing to do, it also may be a wise action at this time. Because Jerry called, Jonathan may next call his contact and put in a good word for Jerry's impending candidacy. After all, Jonathan was sufficiently impressed with Jerry to give him the referral to Jill in the first place. This thank you call confirms Jonathan's wisdom for having referred Jerry to Jill. Similar types of thank you calls are appropriate for other job search occasions, such as thanking someone for useful information and advice. Perhaps someone loaned you a book or counseled you about your job search. Make a thank you follow-up call expressing your appreciation.

Resume or Application Follow-Up

CALLER: *"Hi, this is JoAnna Salem calling in reference to a letter and resume I sent to your office last week for the graphic design position you advertised in the Times. I wanted to check if you received it and if you had any questions."*

RECEIVER: *"Yes, we did get your resume. We're currently reviewing applications. I don't think we have any questions at this time. We'll give you a call if we do."*

CALLER: *"Do you know when you might be making the final decisions?"*

RECEIVER: *"We're trying to complete our review this week. We'll probably start interviewing sometime next week or the week after. I know Mr. Davis wants to get the position filled as soon as possible."*

CALLER: *"I'm really interested in the position. It's a perfect fit with my five years of experience in the publishing industry. Do let me know if you need any additional information. I would be happy to have you talk with several of my clients who know my work well."*

ANALYSIS: While this follow-up call yields some useful information about the decision-making process, it also may give your application added attention. The fact that the receiver had to check to see if they received your resume may help give your resume this attention. And it doesn't hurt to pitch yourself some more for the position. If you sound really good over the phone, the person may move you from the bottom of the pile to the top. You, in effect, conducted a screening interview for the position before being called by the employer for such an interview. This critical call may result in you being remembered more than other candidates. It's important that you not be too pushy when making such a call. You can easily turn off an employer by being too aggressive when making a follow-up call. You don't want to get remembered as a jerk! Get the information, make your point, and get remembered as a professional person who can communicate well with others.

MAKING COLD CALLS FOR UNCOVERING JOB LEADS

Many people use the telephone to randomly uncover job leads. In fact, one approach of job clubs is to use the Yellow Pages to call employers directly to find out if they have vacancies. This type of call basically asks *"Do you have a job for me?"* It's the type of call that results in numerous rejections because (1) most employers contacted do not have vacancies at that particular moment and (2) employers are not keen about broadcasting vacancies to cold callers. Nonetheless, if you don't mind encountering numerous rejections and you are prepared to play the probability game, go ahead and try your luck. You might uncover two appropriate vacancies for every 100 cold calls you make. Your call might go something like this:

CALLER: *"Hi, this is Marcia Voris calling. Do you have any vacancies for word processors?"*

RECEIVER: *"Not at present."*

CALLER: *"Are you accepting applications?"*

RECEIVER: *"You can send us a resume if you wish. We'll keep it on file in case a vacancy would arise at another time. We do periodically hire for such positions."*

CALLER: *"To whom should I address my correspondence?"*

RECEIVER: *"Just send it to the Personnel Department."*

CALLER: *"I would really like to address it to a person."*

RECEIVER: *"It really doesn't matter, but go ahead and send it to Richard Merit who handles our resume bank."*

CALLER: *"Thank you very much for your assistance. By the way, what is your name?"*

RECEIVER: *"Jeffrey Plant. I'm Mr. Merit's assistant."*

ANALYSIS: While we don't put much stock in making these types of cold calls, nonetheless, you can achieve some level of success if you move beyond just identifying vacancies. If you learn there are no vacancies at present, push on to find out about application procedures. Many organizations maintain resume banks which they refer to when vacancies arise. If the company accepts resumes or applications, try to get the name of the person you should contact. In this case, the caller was able to get the name of two people. When she submits her resume to Mr. Merit, she can mention in her letter how helpful Mr. Plant was and that he recommended that she submit her resume for consideration. She now has two contacts and a resume in this organization. Not bad for what was probably a two minute call. If you make 100 such calls in a day, you should be able to collect 100 new names and submit 50 or more resumes.

CALLING IN RESPONSE TO ADS AND VACANCY ANNOUNCEMENTS

You also should network for information relevant to specific job vacancies. Most classified ads or vacancy announcements, for example, outline application procedures. Some may specifically state *"No phone calls please."* Nonetheless, the majority of employers will answer phone calls. Some may even encourage such calls because it indicates an interest in the position and company. At the same time, many applicants will call before they submit a resume and other documents for application. You are well advised to immediately call the company and ask for more information about the position. Read the ad carefully and list the questions you need addressed. You want to gather as much information about both the company and the position so you can "custom design" your resume and letter around the needs of the employer. Your call might go something like this:

CALLER: *"Hi, this is Beverly Rodriguez calling. Your ad in today's Post for a dental assistant caught my attention. I'm thinking about applying, but I need more information. Could you tell me a little more about the position and The Cooper Group?"*

RECEIVER: Responds to question with more information.

CALLER: *"That sounds interesting. You must work for a very exciting organization. I'll definitely submit my application. To whom should I address my resume?"*

RECEIVER: *"Send it to the attention of Tara Marks. She's in charge of handling this position."*

CALLER: *"By the way, do you know when she expects to make the final decision?"*

ANALYSIS: By calling for more information about the position and organization, the caller may gain some useful "inside" information that will give him an advantage over the competition. For example, she might learn that it's a 30-hour a week position with no benefits. She might work with five doctors rather than one. The company may be seeking someone with at least five years of experience. The job might involve traveling to several nursing homes. She might learn about the salary range. In addition, she may get the name of the person handling the screening process and thus better personalize her correspondence. When it comes to follow-up, she has the name of the person to contact and knows when to best call. Needless to say, this phone call may yield some very valuable information that will help you both screen the employer and better develop an employer-centered application.

EFFECTIVE TELEPHONE CLOSINGS

Similar to closing a job search letter, your telephone closing should end in some sort of future action. If you are closing a networking call, you should close with (1) an expression of gratitude, (2) a summary and interpretation of your conversation, and (3) a request for referrals. Your closing might go something like this:

CALLER: (EXPRESS GRATITUDE) *"I really appreciate the information you've given me on marketing opportunities in Eastern Europe and Russia.* (SUMMARIZE AND INTERPRET PREVIOUS CONVERSATION) *You've identified five pharmaceutical companies that seem to have established a strong presence in at least five of these countries. If I understand you correctly, you feel there may be some excellent opportunities with these companies for someone with my interests and skills. I'm especially encouraged by your observation that some of these companies do have entry-level marketing positions overseas.* (REQUEST FOR REFERRALS) *Could I ask one more favor? Do you know two or three other people in this field who would be willing to talk to me about such marketing opportunities?"*

RECEIVER: *"You're quite welcome. Let me think. Yes, why don't you give Mary Sellers at Vialoriate International a call. Her number is 281-0091. John Baird at Southern Pharmaceuticals also would be a good person to contact. His number is 281-1121. It's okay to use my name. I've known them for years. Really good people who know this area well. Tell them I recommended you call them."*

CALLER: *"Thanks so much. Please keep me in mind if you hear of any opportunities for someone with my interests. Would it be okay to send you a copy of my resume for your reference?"*

RECEIVER: *"Sure. I'd be happy to keep it on file and pass it along if I hear of any opportunities."*

CALLER: *"Thanks again. Goodbye."*

ANALYSIS: This is the perfect closing. The job seeker actually managed to turn the closing into two, hopefully three, important actions: (1) received two referrals, (2) got the receiver to accept and read a resume for reference, and (3) requested to be remembered for future referrals which may indeed turn into new job contacts. However, one word of caution. This closing is not complete until it is followed up with a thank you letter which includes a copy of the resume and a request for future referrals. The thank you letter should genuinely express your gratitude for the person's time and information. For examples of such thank you letters, see our ***Job Search Letters That Get Results: 201 Great Examples*** (Impact Publications, 1995).

ANSWERING MACHINE
OR VOICE MAIL MESSAGE

If you use an answering machine or voice mail system to manage your telephone calls, be sure you do so professionally. Nothing is more irritating than to waste people's time with a lengthy voice mail message. Nothing will kill your chances of getting a job quicker than to have an important caller hear an unprofessional or silly message on your answering machine. Keep your answering machine or voice mail message simple, professional, and to the point. This one works well:

> *"Sorry I missed your call. Please leave your name, telephone number, and a message at the sound of the beep. I'll return your call as soon as possible. Thanks for calling."*

When networking by telephone, you can expect to encounter voice mail with at least fifty percent of your calls. More and more people in all types and sizes of organizations use voice mail to collect, screen, and retrieve their messages. When you make a phone call, expect to leave a message on voice mail rather than communicate directly with the individual you are calling. Many voice mail systems put you directly through to the individual's mail box whereas other systems may first route you through an operator or give you an operator option. If you have an operator option, ask the operator when you might best be able to contact the individual directly. He or she may be able to suggest a good time to call back. At the same time, leave a message in the individual's mail box.

Be sure to leave an informative message that is likely to result in a return call. People who use voice mail tend to be busy people who must screen which calls they will return. At least 30 percent of voice mail messages can be disregarded with little or no consequences. Many of these messages are cold calls intended to solicit business and acquire information. Make sure your message does not get screened into that 30 percent! Your message should state the following: (1) the purpose of your call, (2) the best time to contact you, and (3) your phone number. If you fail to clearly state your purpose, you may be screened out as a potential nuisance call. In your statement of purpose, try to connect yourself to the individual's interests. For example,

Referral Connection

"Jim Carlson suggested I call you about your work at ..."

Cold Call

"This is Janice Wilson at 717-234-1100. I'm calling in reference to your work in computer sales."

Expand your statement to include a complete message. A cold call message might include the following:

"Hi, this is Emily Zeiber. I'm calling about your innovative work in graphic design. It's now 1:45pm. I'll be in until 6:00pm today and all day tomorrow. My number is 221-4941. I look forward to speaking with you soon."

Use your own voice mail, an answering machine, an answering service, a beeper, or e-mail if you are difficult to contact by phone. Looking for a job requires constant communication within an ever expanding network. Since you will be making numerous phone calls in developing your job search network, make sure you can be easily contacted. If someone returns your call and gets no answer or no opportunity to leave a message, don't expect that person to call you back again. Returning a call once is sufficient for most people who know little or nothing about you and the purpose of your call. At the very minimum you should use an answering machine or some form of voice mail. If you use the Internet or one of the commercial electronic communication systems, you may want to use your e-mail address in your job search.

When leaving messages on voice mail, make sure your message motivates the receiver to return your call immediately. Most individuals prioritize which messages they will return. Your message should sufficiently grab the attention of the receiver to call you back immediately.

Your message should clearly state who you are and the nature of your call. Be clear and purposeful when leaving messages. Nothing is more irritating than to listen to a message that only includes a name and phone number. If the person does not know who you are or why they should call you back, chances are they will screen out your call. They may assume you are trying to make a cold call to sell them something—calls they wish to avoid!

Your message should ask the receiver to take action—return your call as soon as possible. Again, leaving only a name and telephone number is an incomplete message. Since you want action, your message must call for action. You have two choices here. First, leave a message in which you ask the individual to call you back at such-and-such a time. Second, leave a message in which you indicate you plan to call back at such-and-such a time.

TRY APPROACH LETTERS AND FOLLOW-UP CALLS

You may want to use a more formal approach to gain access to referrals and new contacts. One strategy is to write an approach letter and follow it up with a phone call. Examples of approach letters are found on pages 107-110. These examples are aimed at two different audiences: personal contacts and strangers. The first two letters are written via personal contacts. In the last two examples—"cold turkey" letters—the writers are approaching individuals without prior contacts. In both cases the writers emphasize they are seeking information—not a job—and take the initiative to telephone the individual in order to make an appointment for an informational interview.

As we noted earlier, you should not enclose a copy of your resume with approach letters. The purpose of the letter is to make an appointment for an interview where you will seek job and career information, advice, and referrals. If you enclose a resume with this letter, you will probably send conflicting messages to your audience, that is, you want the person to find you a job.

Your **approach letter** should include the following elements:

Use Appropriate Openers

If you have a referral, tell the individual you are considering a career in _____. His or her name was given to you by ____ _____ who suggested he or she might be a good person to give you useful information about careers in _____.

If you lack a referral to the individual and thus must use a "cold turkey" approach to making contact, you might begin your letter by stating that you are aware he or she has been at the forefront of _____ business—or whatever is both truthful and appropriate for the situation.

APPROACH LETTER: REFERRAL

821 Stevens Points
Boston, MA 01990

April 14, 19___

Terri Fulton
Director of Personnel
TRS Corporation
6311 W. Dover
Boston, MA 01991

Dear Ms. Fulton:

Alice O'Brien suggested that I contact you about my interest in personnel management. She said you are one of the best people to talk to in regard to careers in personnel.

I am leaving government after seven years of increasingly responsible experience in personnel. I am especially interested in working with a large private firm. However, before I venture further into the job market, I want to benefit from the experience and knowledge of others in the field who might advise me on opportunities for someone with my qualifications.

Perhaps we could meet briefly sometime during the next two weeks to discuss my career plans. I have several questions which I believe you could help clarify. I will call your office on Tuesday, April 22, to schedule a meeting time.

I look forward to learning from your experience.

Sincerely,

Katherine Kelly

APPROACH LETTER: REFERRAL

1099 Seventh Avenue
Akron, OH 34522

December 10, 19___

Janet L. Cooper, Director
Architectural Design Office
RT Engineering Associates
621 West Grand Avenue
Akron, OH 34520

Dear Ms. Cooper:

John Sayres suggested that I write to you regarding my interests in architectural drafting. He thought you would be a good person to give me some career advice.

I am interested in an architectural drafting position with a firm which specializes in commercial construction. As a trained draftsman, I have six years of progressive experience in all facets of construction, from pouring concrete to developing plans for $22 million in commercial and residential construction. I am particularly interested in improving construction design and building operations of shopping complexes.

Mr. Sayres mentioned you as one of the leading experts in this growing field. Would it be possible for us to meet briefly? Over the next few months I will be conducting a job search. I am certain your counsel would assist me as I begin looking for new opportunities.

I will call your office next week to see if your schedule permits such a meeting.

Sincerely,

John Albert

APPROACH LETTER:
COLD TURKEY

January 8, 19___

Sharon T. Avery
Vice President for Sales
Bentley Enterprises
529 W. Sheridan Road
Washington, DC 20011

Dear Ms. Avery:

I am writing to you because you know the importance of having a knowledgeable, highly motivated, and enthusiastic sales force to market your fine information processing equipment. I know because I have been impressed with your sales representative.

I am seeking your advice on how I might prepare for a career in your field. I have a sales and secretarial background—experience acquired while earning my way through college.

Within the coming months, I hope to begin a new career. My familiarity with word processing equipment, my sales experience, and my Bachelor's degree in communication have prepared me for the information processing field. I want to begin in sales and eventually move into a management level position.

As I begin my job search, I am trying to gather as much information and advice as possible before applying for positions. Could I take a few minutes of your time next week to discuss my career plans? Perhaps you could suggest how I can improve my resume—which I am now drafting—and who might be interested in my qualifications. I will call your office on Monday to see if such a meeting can be arranged.

I appreciate your consideration and look forward to meeting you.

Sincerely yours,

Gail S. Topper

APPROACH LETTER:
COLD TURKEY

August 29, 19___

Patricia Dotson, Director
Northeast Association for
   the Elderly
9930 Jefferson Street
New York, NY 10013

Dear Ms. Dotson:

I have been impressed with your work with the elderly. Your organization
takes a community perspective in trying to integrate the concerns of the
elderly with those of other community groups. Perhaps other organizations
will soon follow your lead.

I am anxious to meet you and learn more about your work. My background
with the city Volunteer Services Program involved frequent contact with
elderly volunteers. From this experience I decided I preferred working
primarily with the elderly.

However, before I pursue my interest further, I need to talk to people with
experience in gerontology. In particular, I would like to know more about
careers with the elderly as well as how my background might best be used in
the field of gerontology.

I am hoping you can assist me in this matter. I would like to meet with you
briefly to discuss several of my concerns. I will call next week to see if your
schedule permits such a meeting.

I look forward to meeting you and learning from your experience.

Sincerely,

Carol Timms

Make the Request

Demonstrate your thoughtfulness and courtesy rather than aggressiveness by mentioning that you know he or she is busy. You hope to schedule a mutually convenient time for a meeting to discuss your questions and career plans. Most people will be flattered by such a request and happy to talk with you about their work—if they have time and are interested in you.

Close It Right

In closing the letter, mention that you will call the person to see if an appointment can be arranged. Be specific by stating the time and day you will call—for example, *"Thursday at 2pm."* You must take the initiative in this manner and follow-up the letter with a definite contact time. If you don't, you cannot expect to hear from the person. It is **your** responsibility to make the telephone call to schedule a meeting.

Be Careful About Enclosures

Do **not** enclose your resume with this approach letter. You should take your resume to the interview and present it as a topic of discussion near the end of your meeting. If you send it with the approach letter, you communicate a mixed and contradictory message. Remember your purpose for this interview: to gather information and advice. You are not—and never should be—asking for a job. A resume in a letter appears to be an application or a request for a job.

Most people will meet with you, assuming you are sincere. If the person tries to put you off when you telephone for an appointment, clearly state your purpose and emphasize that you are not looking for a job with this person—only requesting information and advice. If the person insists on putting you off, make the best of the situation: try to conduct the informational interview over the phone and request referrals. Follow-up this conversation with a nice thank you letter in which you again state your intended purpose; mention your disappointment in not being able to meet and learn from this person; and ask to be remembered for future reference. You may enclose your resume with this letter.

Many individuals will want to conduct the informational interview over the telephone since he or she is too busy to see you. Such interviews can yield just as good quality information and advice as face-to-face informational interviews. Welcome such interviews since they will save you a great deal of time. When you telephone the person, be prepared to conduct this interview over the phone. Have a list of questions nearby that you planned to ask in the informational interview. Follow-up this telephone interview in the same manner you would follow-up any informational interview—with a thank you letter. You should also enclose your resume with this letter in which you ask to be remembered and referred to others.

Whether you conduct the informational interview in person or over the telephone, treat this interview as an important screening interview. While you are ostensibly seeking information and advice, informational interviews can quickly turn into job interviews should you by chance contact an individual who also has a vacancy or who may create a new position around your qualifications. Therefore, you need to be at your best. Be sure you communicate your competence, intelligence, honesty, and likability in this interview. These are the same qualities you should communicate in a formal job interview.

PREPARE YOUR QUESTIONS

In the informational interview **you** are the interviewer. It is you who is primarily seeking information. Therefore, you need to think through, prior to the interview, several questions you want to probe. For example, you should ask several of these questions:

> *"What type of skills and knowledge does one need to perform this job?"*

> *"What are some of the particular advantages and disadvantages of this type of work?"*

> *"What type of advancement opportunities are there?"*

> *"What is the future outlook like in this line of work?"*

> *"Could you describe a typical work day for me?"*

> *"What do you like about your work?"*

"What do you dislike about your work?"

"What are the normal salary ranges for entry into this type of work?"

"How would I best acquire the necessary skills to perform this job?"

"What type of objections might employers have to my background?"

"What might be the best way to approach prospective employers?"

"How did you go about finding this job?"

Your initial questions should focus on how to improve your job search rather than gather information on the person's company. If, as the interview progresses, it seems appropriate to ask specific questions about the company, go ahead and ask; but be careful. Remember, you are not interviewing for a position with this company—**you are seeking information about a job or career in a given field**. You do not want to wear out your welcome by making the individual feel uncomfortable with questions about a job vacancy this person might have for you. And people do get uncomfortable when you start asking for a job!

CONDUCT THE INTERVIEW WELL

If you approach people in the right manner, at least 50 percent of those you contact for informational interviews will meet with you. Some job hunters are never refused such an interview. Assuming you too are successful in scheduling these interviews, what do you do at the interview?

In the informational interview you want to focus your questions around four outcomes that literally define an effective informational interview:

- Information

- Advice

- Referrals

- To be remembered

At the same time, you are trying to impress upon the people you are interviewing that you possess the essential ingredients for being an outstanding employee: competent, intelligent, honest, enthusiastic, spontaneous, and likable. These are the types of people individuals like to refer to others as well as hire for their own organization.

The interview should take no more than 45 minutes.

While the informational interview is relatively unstructured, it should follow a general pattern of questions and answers. The interview should take no more than 45 minutes. However, it may go much longer if your interviewee gets carried away in sharing his or her experiences and giving you advice. Some interviews may go on for two or more hours. But plan to cover your questions in a 30 to 45 minute period.

For best results, the interview should go something like this. The interview will begin with a few minutes of small talk—the weather, traffic, mutual acquaintances, a humorous observation. Next, you should initiate the interview by emphasizing your appreciation:

> *"Thank you again for taking time to see me today. I appreciate your willingness to speak with me about my career plans. It is a subject which is very important to me at this juncture of my life."*

Follow this statement with a re-statement of your purpose, as you mentioned in your letter and/or over the telephone:

> *"I am in the process of exploring several job and career alternatives. I know what I do well and enjoy doing. But before I make any decisions, I am trying to benefit from the counsel of individuals, such as you, who have a great deal of experience in the area of _____. I am particularly interested in learning more about opportunities, necessary skills, responsibilities, advantages, disadvantages, and the future outlook for this field."*

Such a general statement should elicit a response from the individual. It should put him or her at ease by stressing your need at this time for information and counsel rather than a job.

Be sure you communicate your purpose and that you know what you want to do.

Be sure you communicate your purpose at this stage and that you know what you want to do. If you don't, the individual may feel you are wasting his or her time. Thus, you need to know your strengths as well as have a clearly defined objective **prior to** this interview.

The next section of the interview should focus on several *"how"* and *"what"* questions concerning specific jobs or careers:

- Duties and responsibilities

- Knowledge, skills, abilities, and qualifications

- Work environments—fellow employees, deadlines, stress, problems

- Advantages and disadvantages

- Future outlook

- Salary ranges

Each of these questions can take a great deal of time to answer and discuss. Therefore, prioritize the ones you most need to ask, and try to keep the conversation moving on the various subjects.

Your second major line of questioning should center on your job search. Here you want to solicit useful advice for improving your job search. In relation to the previous job-content questions, you now want to know how to:

- Acquire the required skills

- Find a job related to this field

- Overcome employers' objections to you

- Identify both advertised and unadvertised job vacancies

- Develop new job leads

- Approach prospective employers

Your last major set of questions should deal with your resume. Remember, you have taken copies of your resume to this interview but the person has not seen your resume yet. You have done this purposefully so the individual will get to know you prior to seeing your paper qualifications. At this point you ask the person to critique your resume. Give him or her a copy and ask these questions:

"Is this an appropriate type of resume for the jobs I have outlined?"

"If an employer received this resume in the mail, how do you think he or she would react to it?"

"What do you see as possible weaknesses or areas that need to be improved?"

"What about the length, paper quality and color, layout, and typing? Are they appropriate?"

"How might I best improve the form and content of the resume?"

By doing this, the interviewee will be forced to read your resume—which is a good summary of what you talked about earlier in the interview. Most important of all, he or she will give you useful advice on how to improve and target your resume.

Your last two questions are actually requests to be **referred and remembered**. As you express your gratitude for the person's time, ask for referrals:

"Thanks so much for all your assistance. I have learned a great deal today. Your advice will certainly help me give my job search better

direction. I would like to ask one more favor if I could. By conducting research on various jobs, I am trying to benefit from the counsel of several people. Do you know two or three other people who might be willing to meet with me, as you have today?"

Just before you leave, ask to be **remembered** for future reference:

"While I know you may not know of a job opening at present for someone with my qualifications, I would appreciate it if you could keep me in mind if you learn of any openings. Please feel free to pass my name on to anyone you feel might be interested in my qualifications."

Make sure you leave a copy of your resume with this person so that he or she has something tangible to refer and remember you by.

The examples of dialogues throughout this book are presented to show how one might conduct a phone or face-to-face interview. Certainly you should formulate your strategy in advance of a meeting or phone call. However, under no circumstances should you write out and memorize word-for-word what you plan to say. It will sound memorized and you may even forget and stumble through it. Consider your goals— what you need to convey and what you need to find out—formulate a general plan, make brief notes if you need to, but your conversation should be spontaneous, natural, and enthusiastic.

Let's examine another example of an informational interview as we put all these elements together:

Informational Interview Dialogue

INTRODUCTION: *"Good morning, Mr. Taylor. It's a pleasure to meet you. I really appreciate your taking time to see me and answer some questions that are important to my future."*

PURPOSE AND EXPECTATIONS: *"As I mentioned in my letter, I am exploring diff-different job and career opportunities. The type of work you do interests me very much. I want to learn more about _____ (technical writing, sales, personnel administration). Let me emphasize again that I don't expect you to have or even know of a job vacancy."*

JOB REQUIREMENTS, RELATIONSHIPS, ENVIRONMENTS:

"If it's okay with you, I'd like to ask you some questions about this type of work":

- *"What are some of the regular tasks and activities involved in (occupation)?"*

- *"What skills and abilities are required to do a good job?"*

- *"What kinds of relationships with others are expected or necessary in performing the job?"*

- *"What is the work environment like in terms of pressure, deadlines, routines, and new activities?"*

NOTE: The discussion of work requirements should take 15-20 minutes.

TRANSITION:

"This has been very helpful. You've given me information I've not read nor even considered before."

OCCUPATIONAL OUTLOOK AND APPLICATION ADVICE:

"I'd like to shift the focus a bit and ask your opinion about the future employment outlook in the field of (occupation)":

- *"Are job prospects good, stable, or very competitive?"*

- *"What local organizations employ people in (occupation)?"*

- *"What's the best way to apply for jobs in (occupation)?"*

- *"What is the range for entry-level (or whatever is appropriate) salaries for this type of job?"*

NOTE: Discussion of employment outlook, job hunting, and application procedures should take approximately 10 minutes.

RESUME EVALUATION: *"If you don't mind, could you look at my resume? Perhaps you could comment on its clarity or make suggestions for improving it?"*

- *"Is this resume appropriate for the jobs I've outlined?"*

- *"How do you think an employer would respond to this resume?"*

- *"Do you have any suggestions on how I might strengthen it?"*

NOTE: These questions will force the individual to read your resume and keep a copy for reference and referrals.

OCCUPATIONAL OPPORTUNITIES FOR YOU: *"How would someone with my background get started in (occupation)? What kinds of positions could I qualify for?"*

- *"You've been most generous with your time, and the information you've given me is most useful. It clarifies and reinforces a number of points for me. I have two final requests":*

   "The jobs you thought might be appropriate for someone with my skills sound interesting, and I'd like to find out more about those possibilities. Do you know individuals in those kinds of jobs who would be willing—like yourself—to provide me with additional information?"

NOTE: About half will provide you with multiple referrals.

   "Finally, I would appreciate it if you could keep my resume for reference in case you hear of a vacancy appropriate for someone with my background and interests. Please feel free to pass my name on to others who might be interested in my interests and qualifications."

EXPRESS   *"Thanks again for taking the time to see me.*
GRATITUDE: *You've been very helpful and I appreciate it."*

After completing this interview, you should send a nice **thank you letter** to this person. Not only is this a thoughtful thing to do, it is also a wise thing to do if you wish to be remembered and referred. Genuinely express your gratitude for the person's time and help, and reiterate your wish to be remembered and referred. Page 121 includes an example of such a post-informational interview thank you letter.

PROVIDE USEFUL AND QUALITY INFORMATION

You will often get more honest information in an informational interview than in a job interview. In trying to fill vacancies, employers cannot be objective because they also are attempting to sell you on the benefits of working for them. Informational interviews tend to be less persuasive.

Informational interviews will help you determine if you are interested in a particular career field or job. For example, in our work with college students, we encounter many who aspire to become attorneys. However, a typical conception is based on seeing too many episodes of *L.A. Law* and *Perry Mason*. The image of legal work often is one of standing before the jury dramatically arguing a case. Once these students realize that the two most important skills attorneys use are research and counseling, many quickly lose interest in this career field.

Conducting informational interviews can help you avoid jobs or careers that are not right for you. Whether you are looking forward to a job after you finish school or are already in the workforce but desire to make a job or career change, informational interviews are valuable tools.

EXPECT SERENDIPITY

When conducting informational interviews, you may occasionally un-cover a job opening with the person you are interviewing. Sometimes the company may consider creating a position for you because they are so impressed with your credentials. We have seen this happen with individuals we have counseled. But these are exceptions rather than the rule. Do not go into an informational interview expecting to come out with anything more than information, advice, referrals, and the promise to be remembered.

THANK YOU LETTER

9910 Thompson Drive
Cleveland, OH 43382

June 21, 19___

Jane Evans, Director
Evans Finance Corporation
2122 Forman Street
Cleveland, OH 43380

Dear Ms. Evans:

Your advice was most helpful in clarifying my questions on careers in finance. I am now reworking my resume and have included many of your thoughtful suggestions. I will send you a copy next week.

Thanks so much for taking time from your busy schedule to see me. I will keep in contact and follow through on your suggestion to see Sarah Cook about opportunities with the Cleveland-Akron Finance Company.

Sincerely,

Daryl Haines

FOLLOW PRINCIPLES OF SUCCESSFUL NETWORKING

As you conduct informational interviews and network with many individuals, keep these seven rules in mind:

1. Look for a job that is fit for you rather than try to fit yourself into an available position.

2. Target your job search toward specific positions, organizations, and individuals. Most shot-gun approaches tend to be ineffective.

3. Conduct a persistent prospecting campaign to continually expand your network and replenish contacts that lead to more contacts and informational interviews.

4. Increase your number of acceptances by conducting many informational interviews. When you ask for information, advice, and referrals, few people will turn you down. Most people you ask will be flattered and eager to assist you.

5. If your job search bogs down, chances are you need to substantially increase your daily prospecting activities as well as the number of informational interviews you conduct each week. Persistence, based on an understanding of probability, pays off in the long-run.

6. Always send a thank you letter to those who take the time to talk with you. Thoughtful people tend to be remembered people.

7. In the end, your job search success is a direct function of how well you network according to the principles of prospecting and informational interviewing.

If you follow these simple rules, your networking activities are most likely to turn into actual interviews which lead to offers for high quality jobs.

If you decide not to engage in networking and informational interviews, all is not lost. Each year millions of people do get interviews and job offers by passively submitting applications and resumes in response to vacancy announcements. If you don't network, be prepared to spend a great deal of time on the inherently frustrating advertised job market where you are likely to experience high competition and numerous rejections. Compared to individuals who regularly network for information, advice, and referrals, you'll spend twice as much time looking for a job. And the jobs you find in the advertised job market may not be of the quality you aspire to.

If you want to shorten your job search time, find quality jobs, and target jobs that best fit your particular mix of interests and skills, try networking for information, advice, and referrals.

7

MAINTAINING AND EXPANDING YOUR NETWORK

Networking is not something you should turn on and off, depending on whether you are looking for a job. Networking should become an on-going process both during and after your job search. It should play an important role in advancing your career within and among organizations. But it can only continue playing a role if you pay particular attention to the details of maintaining and expanding your network.

REMEMBER FOLLOW-UP AND FEEDBACK

Effective networkers know the importance of follow-up and feedback both during the job search and once they accept a job offer. They recognize that follow-up and feedback are essential ingredients in the process of maintaining and further expanding their networks.

When you receive a referral from one of your networking contacts, be sure to follow-up the referral with a telephone call. Chances are your contact has already talked to the referral and informed him or her about your interests and indicated that you would contact them soon. Both individuals are expecting you to call. If you fail to follow-up on referral efforts, your contacts may quickly dismiss you as someone who is wasting their time and who is also inconsiderate.

Be sure to follow-up the referral with a telephone call.

When you receive a referral, you should do two things:

- Contact the referral by telephone to arrange a meeting or conduct the informational interview over the phone. Mention in your opening statement that *"Mr. X suggested that I contact you concerning my interest in careers in _____."* In many, but not all, cases your contact will have called this person ahead of time to inform him of your impending call.

- After conducting an informational interview with a referral, contact the source of the referral to thank him for his useful contact. You need to do this in order to emphasize the fact that you indeed did follow-up on the referral and to reemphasize your continuing interest in receiving additional referrals. This is also a good time to provide your contact with feedback on your job search progress. Individuals like to know if their personal efforts produce results. They will remember you for giving them this feedback.

Throughout your job search you will be collecting names, addresses, and phone numbers of individuals who are the subjects of your prospecting, networking, and informational interviewing activities. Once you accept a job offer, be sure to contact individuals in your network who assisted you with information, advice, and referrals. Send them a thoughtful letter in which you (1) inform them of your new position and (2) thank them for their assistance. Individuals who played the most important role in your job search should also receive a phone call from you in which you again inform them of your new position and express your gratitude for their assistance. Sending flowers or a small gift to the most important individuals especially leaves a lasting impression.

Doing follow-up and providing feedback to members of your network is not only a thoughtful thing to do; it is also a wise thing to do. It results in one other important outcome for maintaining and expanding your network in the future: you will most likely be **remembered for future reference**. And this is exactly what you want to do since your new position may be only one of several new positions you acquire during your career. Within another three to five years you may decide it is time to conduct another job search. When that happens, you should have in place a well developed network of individuals who are willing and able to assist you with your job search. If you fail to provide members of your present network with follow-up and feedback, they are less likely to assist you in the future.

NETWORK ON THE JOB

Networking should become a part of your daily routines both on and off the job. Once you begin your new job, remember that your organization is made up of many people who can be helpful in advancing your career within the organization. You should quickly analyze the organizational environment. Learn who has power and influence, whom you should avoid, and who might make a useful mentor, advisor, or friend.

If you want to get ahead on the job, you should run with winners—those who have influence and power to get ahead. Therefore, you will want to continue your prospecting, networking, and informational interviewing activities on the job. However, you must refocus these activities on the career advancement process. What, for example, are the major criteria for getting ahead in this organization? How important is "whom you associate with" to advancing in this organization? Are you associating with the right people and are you clearly communicating your competence, honesty, trustworthiness, enthusiasm, and likability to these individuals? Perhaps more important, are the so-called winners— those you need to run with in order to get ahead—worth the time and effort? You may decide career advancement via such individuals is less than preferable to working elsewhere in the future. The phenomenon of "working for a jerk" is more widespread than many employees have been willing to admit!

Remember, whether we like it or not, all organizations are more or less political in terms of their internal relationships. The sooner you learn about the interpersonal structure of your organization, the sooner you can begin networking with the right people.

DEVELOP LINKAGES TO OTHER ORGANIZATIONS

Regardless of how happy you may be with your present job, there may come a time when you decide it's time to move on to other opportunities in other organizations. You may decide you have advanced as far as possible in Organization X; it's time to look for greener pastures where you can better use your talents. Or you may wish to change careers after deciding you would like to do something else with your life. On a more negative side, you may find yourself on the "outs" with your present employer, experience termination, or are just plain unhappy with your present job. Whatever the positive or negative rationale for looking outside your present organization, there is a 90 percent probability that you will change jobs and careers again within the next 10 years.

If you are like many other people, you suddenly turn off the job search once you find employment. You are no longer concerned with setting career goals, conducting research on organizations, writing resumes, networking, and interviewing. It's only when you are forced to look for a job that you again activate the job search process. When this happens, job seekers find it difficult to get "back into" the job market because their job search skills—especially resume writing and networking—have become so rusty.

Networking should be the one job search skill you keep active while you are employed. Assuming you will one day be looking for another job outside your present organization, it is a good idea to develop, maintain, and expand your networks with professionals in similar types of positions and organizations. You can do this by joining professional organizations. But more important, you should become active in these organizations. For example, many of the associations listed in Chapter Eight are organized at the national and local levels. Local chapters meet regularly to promote their professional interests. They function as networks for exchanging information, advice, and referrals. Many also conduct networking activities and operate job search and placement services for their members.

TRANSCEND THE JOB SEARCH BY BEING IN DEMAND

Have you ever wanted to be in the enviable position of having employers knock on your door rather than you having to always knock on their door? You can achieve a turnaround in the job finding process through your networking activities.

At some point in your career you may be able to transcend the job search process altogether. You do this by achieving a level of recognition that results in other people contacting you with job opportunities. If you can be regularly remembered and referred from other people's networks, you may never need to look for another job because the jobs will come looking for you.

If you network, you may never need to look for another job because the jobs will come looking for you.

Through your regular networking activities, you've come to know numerous individuals who remember your interests, skills, and accomplishments. You've developed mutually supportive professional relations with most people in your immediate and extended network. While your initial networking activities were aimed at expanding the number of people you know, your long-term networking activities result in changing the direction of networking benefits. You'll shift the rules of the hiring game from *"whom you know"* to *"who knows you."* Employers or their representatives—executive search firms, headhunters, and other intermediaries—will knock on your door with questions such as *"Are you interested in making a job change?" "What's your situation with your present employer?" "Are you planning to make any career moves within the foreseeable future?"*

Whatever your professional background or interest, you should join organizations that provide such networking experiences. Active members are those who are also remembered by fellow members. Some are remembered so well that they are often approached by fellow members with new job opportunities. This is the ultimate result of excellent networking: you no longer need to look for a job; you've placed yourself in a position whereby you are in demand by employers. Using their own networking activities, employers, headhunters, and executive search firms come to you with job offers. They try to persuade you to leave your present job to join their organization. Indeed, **if you network well, you may never have to look for another job and engage in a time consuming and often frustrating job search process; instead, the jobs will come looking for you!**

If and when you decide to make a job or career move, fellow members of your association will most likely play a central role in your job search. They will assist you with information, advice, and referrals that should lead to job interviews and offers. In this sense, your next job search should be much easier to conduct than your present one. Your networks will be in place; you merely need to "spread the word" that you are looking for other opportunities. Members of your network should be willing and able to provide you with job leads that will turn into new and exciting opportunities.

8

ORGANIZATIONS AS NETWORKING RESOURCES

Although networking takes place among individuals, formal organizations provide the settings for many networking activities. When looking for employment, you should target your networking toward those organizations that offer job opportunities. When working within an organization, many of your networking activities will take place among co-workers, supervisors, and other influential people within the organization. At the same time, you should maintain linkages with individuals in organizations outside your employer's company.

130

These organizations may consist of professional and trade associations, companies performing similar or competing functions, or community and social groups. All of these organizations are potential sources for your networking activities.

PROFESSIONAL AND TRADE ASSOCIATIONS

Professional and trade associations function as some of the most important networks for finding jobs and advancing careers. These associations operate both inside and outside organizations. Some associations, such as the AFL-CIO, are primarily oriented toward promoting the employment interests of workers by focusing on wages and benefits. Other associations, such as the National Association of Manufacturers, are organized to promote the interests of employers and their companies. All of these organizations provide services to their dues-paying members. These include anything from a monthly magazine and newsletter to insurance, travel, training, and job placement benefits. Indeed, many such associations maintain job bank and referral services, periodically sponsor networking meetings, and provide job search training for their members.

Most important for those seeking employment and advancing careers, professional and trade associations link individuals who work for one employer with individuals who work for other employers. In so doing, they provide a critical communication and networking **bridge** between organizations that assist members in making job and career moves from one organization to another.

INFORMATION SOURCES

You will discover thousands of organizations and associations that perform these linkage functions as well as provide networking opportunities relevant to finding jobs and advancing careers. Most of these organizations can be easily accessed by surveying a few key directories that provide the names, addresses, telephone numbers of—as well as inside information on—these organizations. The two most important directories, both readily available in the reference room of most major libraries, are:

National Trade and Professional Associations (Washington, DC: Columbia Books, annual)

Encyclopedia of Associations (Detroit, MI: Gale Research, annual)

These two directories alone will give you access to more than 25,000 trade and professional associations.

If you are interested in public employment, see Lauber's *The Government Job Finder* (River Forest, IL: Planning/Communication). This book includes a comprehensive listing of publications and organizations that provide job finding services for federal, state, and local government. This book is found in many libraries or it can be ordered directly from Impact Publications.

KEY ASSOCIATIONS

The following listing of organizations is only a sampling of the many thousands of professional and trade associations you will discover as you conduct research on these centers for networking. We include three examples for each category. The categories are organized according to different occupational groups. As you conduct further research, you will discover that engineers, health care workers, insurance professionals, and numerous other occupations have many different associations representing different types of professionals and industries. For example, you will find more than 100 associations for engineers. These associations are specialized according to the type of engineering: cost, chemical, mining, petroleum, civil, gas, naval, mechanical, safety, energy, audio, biomedical, insulated cable, ceramic, packaging, logistic, automotive, broadcast, flight test, explosives, and the list goes on and on. Therefore, you need to specify the type of association appropriate for your particular skills and interests. You can only do this by spending some time researching the various types of trade and professional associations.

While our addresses and telephone numbers relate to the national headquarters, most of these associations also are organized at the state and local levels. Very large associations may, for example, have local chapters centered in major cities and regions. These chapters may publish their own newsletters, meet on a monthly basis, sponsor networking events, and provide job search and placement services to their members. These groups may become your most valuable networking resource.

It would be to your benefit to identify two or more associations relevant to your professional interests. Contact the headquarters office for information on services and membership. If the association has a local chapter, contact a few of the members to find out more about the association. You may be pleasantly surprised to find a group of professionals sharing your interests. If you decide to join, we urge you to get involved by becoming a **participant** in the organization rather than just a dues-paying spectator. Networking via such associations works best when you become noticed by other members because of your participation and involvement in furthering the goals of the organization and thus its members.

THE ORGANIZATIONS

Accounting

American Accounting Association: 5717 Bessie Drive, Sarasota, FL 34223-2319, Tel. 813/921-7747.

Institute of Management Accountants: 10 Paragon Drive, Montvale, NJ 07645-1760, Tel. 201/573-9000.

National Society of Public Accountants: 1010 North Fairfax St., Alexandria, VA 22314-1574, Tel. 703/549-6400.

Advertising

American Advertising Federation: 1101 Vermont Ave., NW, Suite 500, Washington, DC 20005, Tel. 202/898-0089.

American Association of Advertising Agencies: 666 Third Ave., New York, NY 10017-4056, Tel. 212/682-2500.

Association of National Advertisers: 155 East 44th St., New York, NY 10017-4270, Tel. 212/697-5950.

Banking and Finance

American Bankers Association: 1120 Connecticut Ave., NW, Washington, DC 20036, Tel. 202/663-5000.

American Finance Association: New York University, Graduate School of Business, 100 Trinity Place, New York, NY 10006, Tel. 212/998-0370.

National Bankers Association: 1802 T Street, NW, Washington, DC 20009, Tel. 202/588-5432.

Business

Alpha Kappa Psi: 9595 Angola Ct., Indianapolis, IN 46268-1119, Tel. 317/872-1553.

Chamber of Commerce of the United States of America: 1615 H St., NW, Washington, DC 20062-2000, Tel. 202/659-6000.

National Business League: 1511 K Street, NW, Suite 432, Washington, DC 20005, Tel. 202/737-4430.

Chemical Industry

American Chemical Society: 1155 16th St., NW, Washington, DC 20036, Tel. 202/872-4600.

International Chemical Workers Union: 1655 West Market St., Akron, OH 44313, Tel. 216/867-2444.

Oil, Chemical, and Atomic Workers International Union: Box 281299, Lakewood, CO 80228-8200, Tel. 303/987-2229.

Communications

Association for Business Communications: Department of Management, University of North Texas, Denton, TX 76203, Tel. 817/565-4423.

Communications Marketing Association: 9900 Baldwin Place, El Monte, CA 91731-2204, Tel. 303/371-8182.

International Communication Association: 12750 Merit Dr. LB-89, Suite 710, Dallas, TX 75251, Tel. 214/233-3889.

Counseling

American Counseling Association: 5999 Stevenson Ave., Alexandria, VA 22304-3300, Tel. 703/823-9800.

International Association of Addictions and Offender Counseling: 5999 Stevenson Ave., Alexandria, VA 22304, Tel. 703/823-9800.

National Rehabilitation Counseling Association: 8807 Sudley Rd., Suite 102, Manassas, VA 22110-4719, Tel. 703/361-2077.

Data Processing

American Society for Information Science: 8720 Georgia Ave., Suite 501, Silver Spring, MD 20910-3602, Tel. 301/495-0900.

Data Processing Management Association: 505 Busse Highway, Park Ridge, IL 60068, Tel. 708/825-8124.

Society for Information Management: 401 North Michigan Ave., Chicago, IL 60611-4267, Tel. 312/644-6610.

Economics

American Economic Association: 2014 Broadway, Suite 305, Nashville, TN 37203-2418, Tel. 615/322-2595.

Econometric Society: Department of Economics, Northwestern University, Evanston, IL 60208-2600, Tel. 708/491-3615.

National Association of Business Economists: 1233 20th St., NW, Suite 505, Washington, DC 20036, Tel. 202/463-6223.

Education

American Association for Higher Education: One Dupont Circle, Suite 360, Washington, DC 20036, Tel. 202/293-6440.

American Federation of Teachers: 555 New Jersey Ave, NW, Washington, DC 20001, Tel. 202/879-4400.

National Education Association: 1201 16th St., NW, Washington, DC 20036-3290, Tel. 202/833-4000.

Electricity and Electronics

American Electronics Association: 5201 Great American Parkway, Suite 520, Santa Clara, CA 95056, Tel. 408/987-4200.

Electronic Industries Association: 2500 Wilson Blvd., Arlington, VA 22201, Tel. 703/907-7500.

Semiconductor Industry Association: 4300 Stevens Creek Blvd., Suite 271, San Jose, CA 95129-1249, Tel. 408/246-2711.

Engineering

American Society for Engineering Management: P.O. Box 867, Annapolis, MD 21401, Tel. 410/263-7065.

Association of Energy Engineers: 4025 Pleasantdale Rd., Suite 420, Atlanta, GA 30340, Tel. 404/447-5083.

National Society of Professional Engineers: 1420 King St., Alexandria, VA 22314-2794, Tel. 703/684-2800.

Government

American Federation of Government Employees: 80 F St., NW, Washington, DC 20001, Tel. 202/737-8700.

American Federation of State, County, and Municipal Employers: 1625 L St., NW, Washington, DC 20036, Tel. 202/429-1000.

American Society for Public Administration: 1120 G St., NW, Suite 700, Washington, DC 20005, Tel. 202/393-7878.

Health Care and Medicine

American Health Planning Association: 1735 Eye St., NW, Suite 501, Washington, DC 20006, Tel. 202/371-1515.

American Medical Association: 515 N. State St., Chicago, IL 60610, Tel. 312/464-5000.

National Association of Public Hospitals: 1212 New York Ave., NW, Suite 800, Washington, DC 20005, Tel. 202/408-0223.

Insurance

American Insurance Association: 1130 Connecticut Ave., NW, Suite 1000, Washington, DC 20036, Tel. 202/828-7100.

Appraisers Association of America: 386 Park Avenue S., Suite 2000, New York, NY 10016, Tel. 212/899-5404.

National Association of Casualty and Surety Executives: 1130 Connecticut Ave., NW, Suite 1000, Washington, DC 20036, Tel. 202/828-7104.

Management and Personnel

American Management Association: 135 West 50th St., New York, NY 10020-1201, Tel. 212/586-8100.

International Personnel Management Association: 1617 Duke St., Alexandria, VA 22314, Tel. 703/549-7100.

Society for Human Resource Management: 606 N. Washington St., Alexandria, VA 22314, Tel. 703/548-3440.

Nursing

American Health Care Association: 1201 L St., NW, Washington, DC 20005, Tel. 202/842-4444.

American Nurses' Association: 600 Maryland Ave., SW, Suite 100 W., Washington, DC 20024-2571, Tel. 202/651-7000.

National Student Nurses Association: 555 W. 57th St., Suite 1327, New York, NY 10017, Tel. 212/571-2211.

Planning

American Planning Association: 1776 Massachusetts Ave., NW, Suite 400, Washington, DC 20036, Tel. 202/872-0611.

Meeting Professionals International: 1950 Stemmons, Freeway, Infomart Building, Suite 5018, Dallas, TX 75207-3109, Tel. 214/712-7700.

National Planning Association: 1424 17th Street, NW, Suite 700, Washington, DC 20036, Tel. 202/265-7685.

Psychology

American Psychological Association: 750 1st Street, NW, Washington, DC 20002-4242, Tel. 202/336-5500.

Association for the Advancement of Psychology: P.O. Box 38129, Colorado Springs, CO 80937, Tel. 719/520-0688.

National Mental Health Association: 1021 Prince St., Alexandria, VA 22314-2971, Tel. 703/684-7722.

Radio and Television

International Television Association: 6311 N. O'Connor Rd., LB-51, Irving, TX 75039, Tel. 214/869-1112.

National Association of Broadcasters: 1771 N Street, NW, Washington, DC 20036, Tel. 202/429-5300.

Screen Actors Guild: 5757 Wilshire Blvd., Los Angeles, CA 90036-3600, Tel. 213/549-6400.

Real Estate

National Association of Mortgage Brokers: 706 E. Bell Road, Suite 101, Phoenix, AZ 85022, Tel. 602/992-6181.

National Association of Realtors: 430 N. Michigan Ave., Chicago, IL 60611, Tel. 312/329-8200.

Property Management Association: 8811 Colesville Rd., Suite G106, Silver Spring, MD 20910, Tel. 301/587-6543.

Social Work

National Association for Home Care: 519 C Street, NE, Stanton Park, Washington, DC 20002, Tel. 202/547-7424.

National Association of Social Workers: 750 First St., NE, Suite 700, Washington, DC 20002-4241, Tel. 202/408-8600.

Sports

National Association of Sports Officials: 2017 Lathrop Ave,. Racine, WI 53405, Tel. 414/632-5448.

National Sportscasters and Sportswriters Association: Box 559, Salisbury, NC 28144, Tel. 704/633-4275.

Sporting Goods Manufacturers Association: 200 Castlewood Dr., North Palm Beach, FL 33408, Tel. 407/842-4100.

Transportation

American Public Transit Association: 1201 New York Ave., NW, Suite 400, Washington, DC 20005, Tel. 202/898-4000.

International Brotherhood of Teamsters: 25 Louisiana Ave., NW, Washington, DC 20001, Tel. 202/624-6800.

Transport Workers Union of America: 80 West End Avenue, New York, NY 10023, Tel. 212/873-6000.

Several other associations are organized around various population groups, such as women and minorities, that have professional interests. These organizations may cross-cut occupational fields or they may group women and minorities within a particular profession or industry. Examples of such organizations for both women and minorities include the following:

Women

American Business Women's Association: 9100 Ward Parkway, P.O. Box 8728, Kansas City, MO 64114, Tel. 816/361-6621.

Association for Women in Science: 1522 K Street, NW, Suite 820, Washington, DC 20005, 202/408-0742.

Women's Education and Leadership Forum: 1335 P Street, NW, Suite 300, Washington, DC 20005, Tel. 703/352-0551.

Minorities

American Association for Affirmative Action: 8335 Allison Pointe Tr., No. 250, Indianapolis, IN 46250, Tel. 317/841-8038.

American Indian Health Care Association: 1550 Larimer St., No. 225, Denver, CO 80202-1602, Tel. 303/293-9128 or 303/295-3757.

National Association of Black Owned Broadcasters: 1333 New Hampshire Avenue, NW, Suite 1000, Washington, DC 20036, Tel. 202/463-8970.

JOB SEARCH NETWORKING ORGANIZATIONS

Several organizations function as networking groups for individuals seeking employment. Ostensibly known as job clubs and networking groups, most are organized to provide job search assistance for a particular population group, such as women, minorities, military personnel, alumni, mid-career individuals, or retirees. If, for example, you are over 40 years old and unemployed, you should consider joining a Forty Plus Club nearest you. The Forty Plus Clubs are self-help support groups that operate like job clubs. Members pay a monthly fee to join and participate in the day-to-day operation of the organization. They use club facilities to conduct job research, telephone prospective employers, attend job search meetings, and provide mutual support to other club members. At present 21 Forty Plus Clubs operate in ten states and the District of Columbia:

CALIFORNIA

7440 Lockheed Street
Oakland, CA 94603
Tel. 510/430-2400

1150 N. First, #201
San Jose, CA 95110
Tel. 408/288-3555

3450 Wilshire Boulevard
Los Angeles, CA 90010
Tel. 213/388-2301

23172 Plaza Point Dr.
Laguna Hills, CA 92553
Tel. 714/581-7990

8845 University Center Lane
San Diego, CA 92122
Tel. 619/450-4440

COLORADO

3842 S. Mason Street
Fort Collins, CO 80526
Tel. 303/223-2470

2555 Airport Road
Colorado Springs, CO 80910
Tel. 719/473-6220, ext. 271

800 W. Alameda Avenue
Lakewood, CO 80026
Tel. 303/223-2470

HAWAII

126 Queen Street, #227
Honolulu, HI 96813
Tel. 808/531-0896

MINNESOTA

14870 Granada #315
St. Paul, N 55124
Tel. 612/683-9898

NEW YORK

15 Park Row
New York, NY 10038
Tel. 212/233-5086

701 Seneca Street
Buffalo, NY 14210
Tel. 716/858-0491

OHIO

1100 King Avenue
Columbus, OH 43212
Tel. 614/297-0040

PENNSYLVANIA

1218 Chestnut St.
Philadelphia, PA 19107
Tel. 215/923-2074

TEXAS

13140 Colt Rd., #300
Dallas, TX 75240
Tel. 214/783-2300

2909 Hillcroft, #400
Houston, TX 77057
Tel. 713/952-7587

UTAH

5735 S. Redwood Road
Murray, UT 84123
Tel. 801/269-4797

480 27th Street
Ogden, UT 84409
Tel. 801/399-2181

1550 N. 200 West
Provo, UT 84503
Tel. 801/373-7500

WASHINGTON STATE

300 120th Ave., NE, #7
Bellevue, WA 98005
Tel. 206/450-0040

WASHINGTON, DC

1718 P Street, NW
Washington, DC 20036
Tel. 202/387-1582

Since additional Forty Plus Clubs are being formed in other states, you may want to check your local phone book to see if a chapter has been formed in your area or call the New York City Forty Plus Club (Tel. 212/233-6086) for more information. In the process of doing so, you may discover other types of self-help networking groups (look for Experience Unlimited Job Clubs in California or The Five O'Clock Club in New York City), from women's centers to church groups, formed for assisting individuals with the job search process. In fact, each week the *National Business Employment Weekly* (available at many newstands or call 800-JOB-HUNT) lists the activities of such groups in various communities across the country in its column called "Calender of Career Events."

If you are separating from the military, you should consider joining one of the two major military retirement groups. Each group maintains a placement service which provides a variety of useful job search and placement services to its members, from networking activities to computerized resume banks. Retired officers will want to join

The Retired Officers Association (TROA)
201 N. Washington Street
Alexandria, VA 22314-2529
Tel. 800/245-8762 or 703/838-8117

An annual membership in TROA costs $20. TOPS, which is TROA's Officer Placement Service, provides the following career transition services: job/career counseling, resume critique, job search lectures and workshops, reference library, candidate database for matching candidates with employers, and a complimentary copy of TROA's job search/resume guide, *Marketing Yourself for a Second Career*. TOPS especially promotes the importance of networking in the job search.

Non commissioned officers should consider joining the **Non Commissioned Officers Association (NCOA)**. This organization operates the Veterans Employment Assistance (VEA) Program. Through this program NCOA offers free Career Transition Seminars and Job Seekers Workshops worldwide. It also sponsors job fairs in the U.S. and Europe, an online database for matching candidates' qualifications with employers' hiring needs, and resume writing assistance. For information and membership, contact

Non Commissioned Officers Association
10635 IH 35 North
San Antonio, TX 78233
Tel. 210/753-6161

The cost of an annual membership is $20.00.

Two other military associations provide career transition and networking services to its members. The **Armed Forces Communications and Electronics Association (AFCEA)** can be contacted at the following address:

**AFCEA (Armed Forces Communications
    and Electronics Association)**
4400 Fair Lakes Court
Fairfax, VA 22033-3899
Tel. 800/336-4583, ext. 6144 or 703/631-6144

AFCEA's Career Planning Center offers resume preparation and referral assistance and organizes career transition seminars and job fairs for its members. The cost of annual membership in AFCEA is $20.00.

The **Association of the United States Army (AUSA)** also offers career transition services to its members. For information on membership in AUSA, contact

Association of the United States Army
2425 Wilson Boulevard
Arlington, VA 22201-3385
Tel. 703/841-4300

AUSA's career transition program is handled separately:

AUSA Transition Assistance Program
Suite 206
3500 Virginia Beach Boulevard
Virginia Beach, VA 23452
Tel. 804/486-2155 or 800/233-1280

Women entering or re-entering the job market will find several organizations providing them with job search and networking assistance. Sponsored by local governments, community colleges, or colleges and universities, women's centers often maintain career libraries, offer job search workshops, and sponsor networking events for women seeking employment. More than 2,000 such organizations are associated with the National Network of Women's Employment (formerly known as the Displaced Homemakers Network). For information on a member organization nearest you, contact:

National Network of Women's Employment
1625 K Street, NW, Suite 300
Washington, DC 20006
Tel. 202/467-6346

For a comprehensive review of resources—from reference books and directories to professional associations, employment services, and networking groups relevant to hundreds of different professional and population groups—we highly recommend that you refer to the current editions of two big career directories published by Gale Research (Detroit, Michigan):

Job Hunter's Sourcebook (Michelle Le Compte, ed.)

Professional Careers Sourcebook (Kathleen M. Savage and Joseph M. Palmisano, eds.)

You should also examine the latest editions of Dan Lauber's two directories which are designed for professionals and those interested in working with nonprofit organizations. Packed with hundreds of networking resources and job leads, both books are published by Planning/Communications in River Forest, Illinois:

The Nonprofits' Job Finder

The Professional's Private Sector Job Finder

Each volume includes information on job services, key directories, salaries, and job vacancies for individuals interested in networking for job information, advice, and leads.

All of these books are available in most public libraries or they can be ordered directly from Impact Publications (see order form at end of this book).

9

NEW
ELECTRONIC
NETWORKING

The 1990s has witnessed a virtual revolution in networking with the advent of computerized databases and online employment services. Collectively known as "electronic networking," these databases and services are literally designed to create new networks of job seekers and employers. Some charge a yearly or per service fee while others are free to job seekers. Most are financed by venture capitalists in search of new profit centers and/or employers who use the services to list vacancies and recruit candidates. Some are relatively passive networks requiring little or no effort on your part, other than joining a network

146

operated by a job listing service. Others require you to take a great deal of initiative in shaping your own network by acquiring information, advice, and referrals and developing employment contacts through participation in online "chat groups" or "news groups" via e-mail. Your online sleuthing and writing skills will largely determine your degree of online networking success.

For individual job seekers, these electronic databases and online services enable them to quickly and conveniently conduct research on jobs and employers, acquire job information and advice, access employment data, post resumes online, and continuously target a job search toward numerous employers nationally as well as internationally. Many of the databases and services enable individuals to broadcast their resumes to thousands of potential employers who would not have been reached through more traditional job search or networking methods. These forms of electronic networking also give new meaning to the "information interview" which can be conducted with hundreds of individuals who participate in chat groups, use electronic bulletin boards, and communicate by e-mail. Best of all, electronic networking can be conducted 24 hours a day, 7 days a week, and 365 days a year from your home or office.

THE REVOLUTION IS NOW

Like other revolutions, the electronic job search revolution seems to be based on a vision and a great deal of hype. It goes something like this. Electronic networking is one of the fastest growing job search methods and mediums in today's job market. Within the next ten years electronic networks may transform the way job seekers market themselves to potential employers and the way employers recruit candidates. Working from their personal computers or through computerized job search services with extensive electronic resume and employer banks, job seekers will be able to quickly broadcast their qualifications to thousands of employers and acquire useful job market information. No longer will many people need to spend three, six, or nine months pounding the pavement, responding to classified job ads with mailed cover letters and resumes, attending meetings, making cold telephone calls, contacting strangers, or scheduling face-to-face informational interviews. Indeed, some of the traditional networking methods outlined in this book may become obsolete, or perhaps dramatically transformed, in this new electronic job search era. This revolution is likely to put many traditional job search providers out of business.

Since electronic networking methods are likely to cut job search time by 50 to 70 percent, they should prove to be a cost effective way of linking candidates to employers. Employers may find they cost less and generate better quality candidates than the more traditional recruitment methods of placing classified ads, hiring employment firms, or broadcasting vacancy announcements. Job seekers will discover that electronic networking enables them to quickly reach a very broad sample of employers that would not be available through other job search methods.

PROMISES FOR PARADISE

Electronic networking will quickly become one of the most efficient and effective ways of matching qualified candidates to employers. It will displace many current inefficient and ineffective employment services. Traditional networking methods will become less important in this new electronic job search era. Indeed, electronic networking may make many traditional job search techniques obsolete.

At the heart of this revolution is the issue of money—who pays for it and who will reap the financial rewards?

At least these seem to be the promises in this new era of electronic networking. Behind much of the hype about electronic networking is the fact that this is largely an unchartered frontier for both employers and job seekers which has yet to prove its effectiveness and long-term viability. At the heart of this revolution is the issue of money—who pays for it and who will reap the financial rewards of controlling access to the new electronic networks? So far much of this electronic revolution has been presented to job seekers as a free lunch, but someone must finance it; that someone is mostly employers who are being enticed into these electronic networks with promises of extraordinary yet unseen benefits. Other likely financiers will be the same employment sharks who have a long history of taking advantage of job seekers by charging them for questionable job finding services; these sharks are now acquiring online skills to reap new benefits. Their game is the same but merely transferred to a new medium.

To the disappointment of many entrepreneurs shaping these new electronic networks, no one seems to be making much money nor has anyone found a good formula to sustain profitability in the long-run. As a result, the electronic revolution is a bit like the proverbial sailboat—investor money seems to go into a big black hole. In the end, the sharks may gain a major foot-hold in this medium for marketing their questionable services.

The electronic job networking revolution has evolved so fast, and constantly changing its shape from day-to-day, that no one can say for certain where it is at present nor exactly where it is going over the next year or two or beyond. We do know electronic networking shares one characteristic with the traditional job market—a truly chaotic arena. However, several new cautionary "facts of life" have emerged relevant to this new electronic revolution:

1. **Several resume database firms that led this revolution just two or three years ago (kiNexus, Connexion, Career Placement Registry) have either gone out of business or transformed their operations** to be compatible with the latest electronic trends—the use of the Internet and e-mail, two "nonprofit" centers for businesses. A highly competitive arena for high-tech entrepreneurs in search of content, electronic employment networks have not been profitable operations for most companies venturing into this arena; most must resign themselves with the expectation that this will be a long-term investment with a few "winners" emerging in perhaps five or ten years from now. Indeed, no one has figured out how to make much money operating these databases and services, beyond charging employers for listing job vacancies and conducting candidate searches—traditional advertising and recruitment functions that used to be monopolized by newspapers and employment firms; individual job seekers have not been good paying customers. And these two ostensible profit centers (databases and services) may be in the process of disappearing altogether as more and more employers and job seekers use the free access of the Internet for electronic employment networking. Thus, we expect more and more electronic database and employment firms to emerge as well as go out of business within the next year or two as the

Internet emerges as the center for free electronic networking. Except for those that perform highly specialized recruitment functions, we do not expect many for-profit employment database and service firms to survive beyond 1998; few will enter the 21st century. The continuing fall-out of such services and firms looks inevitable in what appears to be continuing chaos in cyberspace.

2. **Most of what you may have read about the electronic job search revolution six months ago is probably obsolete by now** because of the rapid changes taking place in this new employment arena. Even what we say here in this chapter on electronic networking will probably be obsolete within the next few months. No one is sure where it is going, but the current chaos seems to be going anywhere but North! As one of the leading electronic job search experts, Joyce Lain Kennedy, recently observed, in the long-run job seekers are best off learning how to use the Internet and e-mail for electronic networking—electronic skills that will serve them well in the job markets of today and tomorrow. Everything else may be a short-term distraction. Indeed, right now we're seeing lots of cowboys in cyberspace trying to stake out profitable businesses that have yet to bear fruit. Most will not survive long as they continue to fall out in the face of harsh economic realities in the new electronic age—can't figure out how to turn a profit in both the short-run and long-run.

3. **The effectiveness of new electronic networking over traditional interpersonal networking has yet to be proven nor are they necessarily in competition with each other.** The hype and hoopla about electronic networking is based on a vision or promise rather than on concrete performance. As with any self-proclaimed revolution, there is a tendency to get seduced by a vision of the future, lose perspective, and thus confuse promises with performance as well as the media with the message. It's true that some employers do recruit candidates, and some job seekers do find jobs using electronic databases, online services, and the Internet, but no one knows to what extent they do. One suspects the numbers are very low, and for good reasons. So far the technology has been primarily applied to and hyped for the least effective job

search activity—broadcasting resumes to employers. This is about the dumbest job search activity anyone can engage in. It simply doesn't work in over 95 percent of the cases. Not to be dissuaded from such realities, proponents of electronic networking primarily outline the promises and mechanics of using the databases and services. The evidence of performance is largely anecdotal and most of it points in one direction—electronic networking is most effective for employers and job seekers in high-demand high-tech fields or those seeking individuals with an exotic combination of skills and experience. Ironically, the anecdotal evidence tends to reinforce what we've known all along about job listings or the advertised job market—aside from the newness of the technology, there is nothing magical nor new about this revolution in reference to job search and recruitment functions. This new electronic revolution operates similarly to classified ads and executive search firms—it lists jobs and recruits for high-demand positions. Its real advantage is that it does it faster and thus saves both employers and job seekers time and money. The result may be that less than 5 percent of all jobs will be represented through the electronic databases and services. There is little evidence that electronic networking is very effective for individuals seeking entry-level positions outside the current high-demand high-tech fields.

4. **There's a tendency to confuse the medium with the message.** The networking message remains the same: how to best develop job leads and communicate your qualifications to potential employers. An effective job search accomplishes this by connecting with jobs that best "fit" the interests and skills of the job seeker. In the past, the main mediums for doing this have been the mail, telephone, fax, and face-to-face meetings. The new electronic revolution now allows individuals to use computers and online services to quickly acquire job information, identify potential employers, and communicate qualifications to employers by electronic means. It's like having a typewriter connected to a telephone with the capacity to interactively communicate with a vast audience. So far there is little evidence that the new medium will substantially alter the traditional job search message—communication between employer and job seeker.

5. **Despite the hype, false starts, and current chaos, there's no question about it—electronic networking is here to stay and in a very big way.** More and more employers will list their vacancies online and use specialized electronic recruitment services. The main casualties of this electronic revolution will probably be (1) newspapers whose classified ad sections will continue to decline in both size and revenue as more and more of their print business goes online; (2) employment firms and career counselors who do not adapt to the new technology; and (3) several employment database firms and services that failed to move to the Internet as well as failed to solve the issue of profitability on the Internet. The main beneficiaries will be both employers and job seekers who should be able to substantially cut their time and costs in navigating an increasingly competitive and chaotic job market. Our advice to job seekers is to learn how to network both interpersonally and electronically. Learn how to use both the Internet and e-mail as you develop your repertoire of networking skills. You'll need to do both interpersonal and electronic networking for the 21st century!

WHERE IS THE REVOLUTION?

What exactly is this electronic revolution in relation to networking and the job search? During the past three years, it has taken on several forms. One of its most basic and popular forms involves linking job seekers with employers through an electronic resume. Job seekers develop an electronic resume which is capable of being scanned into a sophisticated computerized database consisting of employers who specify qualifications they seek in candidates. In its optimal form, the electronic resume is designed with keywords in mind. For a per search and/or yearly membership fee, employers request one or more of these firms to identify a specific number of candidates who meet their vacancy requirements. The requirements, in the form of keywords, are inputted into the resume bank.

Depending on both the size of the database and the requirements of the employer, this electronic search procedure may generate anywhere from 10 to 50 resumes of potentially qualified candidates. The resumes are then sent to employers who, in turn, review them and select the best ones for initial computer or telephone screening interviews which may eventually turn into a series of job interviews and the selection of one candidate.

The beauty of this electronic job search system is its speed, cost, and effectiveness for both employers and job seekers. While employers may normally spend $1,000 to $20,000, as well as one to three months recruiting an employee, they may accomplish the same goal within one to two weeks at the cost of $100 to $300 by using the services of an electronic resume bank. While job seekers must learn to write a new type of resume—an electronic resume peppered with keywords that are most responsive to this type of technology—the results may be extremely worthwhile and may well revolutionize the whole concept of job seeking. Whether or not they are actively seeking employment, for a yearly membership fee of $30 to $100, individuals can keep their resume in an electronic resume bank. They will be contacted by member employers if and when their resume "matches" the requirements of employers.

Other popular forms of the electronic job search revolution involve career centers and services available through commercial online services (America Online, CompuServe, Delphi, GEnie, Prodigy, Microsoft) and on the Internet (World Wide Web). Here, job seekers can conduct research on jobs and employers, join discussion groups, attend workshops, acquire information and advice from career counselors and fellow job seekers, review thousands of job listings, and transmit resumes to employers. Traditional networking activities, which normally are done over the telephone or in face-to-face meetings, can be conducted through e-mail with hundreds of individuals who volunteer information and advice. Whether or not this is the same quality information and advice acquired through more traditional targeted networking activities is another story altogether. Nonetheless, it is another medium through which you can network for information, advice, and referrals.

JOB HUNTING THAT NEVER STOPS

The revolutionary aspects of this new technology may eventually go far beyond just the electronic matching process that quickly and cost effectively links employers with job seekers. Given the "membership" nature of some electronic databases, they may well revolutionize the way individuals think about their job and career future. The notion that an individual stops job hunting after he or she finds a job will likely be replaced with a new and continuous concept of job hunting: you are always on the lookout for better job opportunities. Paying your annual membership fee and regularly updating your resume for the electronic database, your resume is always working the job market even though ostensibly you are not job hunting. You, in effect, can network 24 hours a day, 7 days a week, and 365 days a year.

Some services enable you to network
24 hours a day, 7 days a week,
365 days a year.

The electronic job search may alter the way people think about the job hunting process. You no longer just turn it on or off when you are in need of another job. It's always turned on. Anytime of the day you can literally surf the Internet for potential job openings. On the other hand, while you may be perfectly content with your current job, as a member of XYZ Job Bank, you regularly hear from employers who are interested in your qualifications. You examine the competition and assess whether or not this is the time for you to make another career move. For you and thousands of other members of XYZ Job Bank, you are always prepared to make strategic job and career moves because you are literally wired so you can electronically network 24 hours a day. Unemployment, job dissatisfaction, and unexpected career shocks are not part of your career perspective or experience. Your continuous career health requires you to always be in the job market by way of your membership in XYZ Job Bank. In fact, you are likely to become a lifetime member of this organization. Over a 40-year worklife period, you may have found 10 of your employers through your membership in XYZ Job Bank. At the cost of $50 a year, this electronic job service was well worth the expense. Best of all, it reduced the anxiety of having to look for employment under adverse circumstances and through traditional job search methods that were extremely inefficient and ineffective.

Join an electronic job service and your job search will never end! That's if these electronic networks actually get used by employers and job seekers to the degree envisioned by proponents of these new employment networks. The performance evidence remains anecdotal at best.

WHO ARE THE NEW
REVOLUTIONARIES?

During the past few years numerous firms have gotten into the electronic resume and employment businesses. Many of them use electronic e-mail, online bulletin boards, and existing commercial online computer services such as America Online, CompuServe, Prodigy, and Microsoft. Others are accessed solely through the Internet via the World Wide Web. Primarily funded by large Fortune 1,000 corporations, membership in the electronic employment database companies includes individuals, professional associations, and alumni, retirement, military and other groups who are interested in linking electronic resumes to member companies. These electronic resume services have become new employer-employee networks which are redefining certain segments of the job market. The marketplace is no longer confined to the classified ads, employment firms, or executive search firms. It is also found in computerized databases developed by electronic resume firms. These firms may bring together over 100,000 members into an electronic network which is constantly seeking to find "good fits" between the needs of employers and the keywords appearing on members' electronic resumes.

The electronic resume services have become new employer-job seeker networks which are redefining segments of the job market.

One of the major advantages of participating in these electronic networks is that you may have access to numerous positions that are not advertised outside the network. When a vacancy occurs or new position is created, participating employers may first turn to the network for qualified candidates before advertising the position outside the electronic network. It may be to your advantage to participate in such a network because you will have access to numerous positions and employers you might not otherwise reach through other networking means.

RESUME DATABASES

Resume databases are the most passive electronic networking activities you can engage in. All you need to do is contact a database firm, submit a resume or complete a candidate profile form, and perhaps pay a monthly or yearly membership fee (some are free because employers buy the tariffs). The firm inputs your resume or personal profile information in the computer along with thousands of other resumes. Employers either have online access to the database or they have the firm conduct candidate searches by screening resumes on specific position criteria. Employers often pay yearly membership fees or per search fees in order to use these databases. All the individual job seeker needs to do is submit a resume or complete a profile form and in some cases pay a fee. Since the resume database firm manages the electronic networking process, all the job seeker needs to do is join the network, similar to joining other types of subscription-based organizations. The job seeker then waits to see what will transpire as the computer attempts to match individual resumes with employer needs. These new resume database systems are high-tech versions of the old resume broadcast method.

These are very volatile businesses still attempting to resolve the issue of profitability, especially in the face of increased competition and the role of the Internet which has quickly become the major medium for electronic networking. Indeed, several major companies that pioneered such databases have gone out of business during the past two years: kiNexus, Connexion, and Career Placement Registry. More are likely to do so within the next few years.

At present, some of the largest and most popular electronic resume database firms include the following:

❑ **Career Net Graduate:** 643 W. Crosstown Parkway, Kalamazoo, MI 49008, Tel. 616-344-3017. Designed for college students and recent graduates, this service puts resumes on CD-ROM discs and distributes them to nearly 10,000 major employers. Charges less than $100 for one academic year; allows two updates.

❑ **Cors:** One Pierce Place, Suite 300 East, Itasca, IL 60143, Tel. 800-323-1352, 708-250-8677 or Fax 708-250-7362. Includes more than 1 million resumes in its database. Contacts with employers to recruit candidates from database. Charges one-time $25 fee for entering resume in database. Allows unlimited updates. Also performs fee-based job search services for job seekers.

❑ **Electronic Job Matching:** 1915 N. Dale Mabry Highway, Suite 307, Tampa, FL 33607, Tel. 813-879-4100 or Fax 813-870-1883. Includes applicant resumes in database that can be accessed by employers who pay search fees. Free of charge for job seekers.

❑ **Gonyea & Associates, Inc.:** 3543 Enterprise Road East, Safety Harbor, FL 34695, Tel. 813-725-9600. Offers several types of electronic services for job seekers. Its Help-Wanted-USA database includes classified employment ads from over 50 major newspapers. The database can be accessed free of charge (less access fees) through America Online or the Internet. The company also on a weekly basis will match your goals to specific job listings or send you the database on a disk for $39.95 for six weeks.

❑ **Mainstream Job Bank USA:** 20 Signal Road, Stamford, CT 06902, Tel. 800-296-1USA or Fax 203-353-1809. Formerly operated as Job Bank USA, this newly reorganized company provides both on-line and off-line career services. You can enter your resume in their database free of charge by transmitting it by e-mail or by sending it on disk. They will scan your resume for a fee. Includes a resume review and career counseling service.

❑ **National Resume Bank:** 3637 4th Street North, No. 330, St. Petersburg, FL 33704, Tel. 813-896-3694 or Fax 813-894-1277. This online resume database includes more than 3,000 resumes for 35 job categories. Employers access the database to match job requirements with specific resumes. Job seekers pay a $40 one-time fee. Employers get free access to database..

❑ **Resume-Link:** 3972-C Brown Park Drive, Hilliard, OH 43026, Tel. 714-777-4000 or Fax 614-771-5708. Specializes in the computer and engineering fields. Includes 20,000+ resumes in its database. Free to job seekers who belong to a relevant professional society ($50 a year for nonmembers). Employers pay.

❑ **SkillSearch:** 3354 Perimeter Hill Drive, Suite 235, Nashville, TN 37211-4129, Tel. 615-834-9448 or Fax 615-834-9453. Sponsored by 60 university alumni associations, alumni associated with each sponsoring university can have their resumes included in the database for $65 the first year and $15 for each additional year. Employers pay a per-search fee to use the database.

❑ **University ProNet:** 2445 Faber Place, Box 51820, Palo Alto, CA 94303, Fax 415-845-4019 (for telephone numbers of each participating alumni group). Participation restricted to alumni of 16 member universities: California Institute of Technology, Carnegie-Mellon University, Columbia University, Cornell University, Massachusetts Institute of Technology, Ohio State University, Stanford University, University of California at Berkeley, University of California at Los Angeles, University of Chicago, University of Illinois, University of Michigan, University of Pennsylvania, University of Texas at Austin, and Yale University. Employers pay an annual subscription fee to participate in database. Alumni charged a one-time $35 registration fee. Operated by the alumni associations at each participating university.

❑ **V-Quest:** 5700 Fourth St. North, St. Petersburg, FL 33703, Tel. 813-528-4005 or Fax 813-528-4406. Provides resumes online to 500 major employers free of charge. Individuals pay $79.95 for the first year to have their personal profile/resume placed in the database.

ONLINE SERVICES

Opportunities for more active forms of electronic networking are found through e-mail, discussion groups, workshops, and career centers of online commercial services or on the Internet's rapidly developing World Wide Web. The major commercial online services with career segments offering electronic networking opportunities include:

❑ **America Online:** 8619 Westwood Center Dr., Vienna, VA 22182, Tel. 800-827-6364 or Fax 703-556-3750. Today's fastest growing and most popular commercial online service claiming a membership of over 4 million users. Its popular America Online's Career Center, operated by James C. Gonyea, offers a variety of useful job search options, from career counseling and chat groups to job listings and career resources. The service also offers other opportunities to network through its chat groups (*People's Connection*), message boards (*The Exchange Message Boards*). and special interest groups and networks for educators, health professionals, lawyers, writers, seniors, and others.

❑ **CompuServe:** 5000 Arlington Centre Boulevard, P.O. Box 20212, Columbus, OH 43220, Tel. 800-848-8199 or Fax 614-457-0348. Claiming more than 3 million subscribers, this popular commercial online service is perhaps the most sophisticated of the bunch. It includes numerous forums and databases from which job seekers can explore job opportunities, exchange information and advice, and conduct research on employers. Its more than 700 forums constitute a rich resource for networking with thousands of individuals who might provide useful information, advice, and referrals.

❑ **Delphi:** Tel. 800-695-4005. This relatively new service offers excellent opportunities to network electronically through various forums and discussion groups relevant to specific professional or career interest groups. *The Job Complex* forum, for example, includes lots of useful job search information, including job listings. Nurses should explore *The Nursing Network* for information on nursing opportunities. And if you really don't want to work for someone else, try *The Self-Employment* forum for tips on starting your own business.

❑ **Dialog:** 3460 Hillview Avenue, Palo Alto, CA 94304, Tel. 800-334-2564 or Fax 415-858-7069. This online information service functions like a big library which provides access to hundreds of newspapers, journals, magazines, and newsletters. It's especially useful for conducting research on various career fields. It includes hundreds of databases on a variety of subjects including government, law, chemistry, economics, engineering, biology, agriculture, and science and technology. You won't find career centers or discussion groups here.

❑ **Genie:** 401 North Washington Street, Rockville, MD 20850, Tel. 800-638-9636. One of the smaller and more struggling online services, GEnie includes a job bank, which is operated by E-Span, as well as the *Business Resource Directory*, the *Home Office/Small Business RoundTable,* and *Dr. Job*, a Q&A forum.

❑ **Microsoft Network:** Microsoft Corporation, 1 Microsoft Way, Redwond, WA 98052, Tel. 800-386-5550. One of the newest and most aggressive online services operated by the Microsoft Corporation and bundled in its Windows 95 software. Includes the

Mainstream Career Center which offers job listings and a variety
of services operated by numerous vendors who offer a combination of free and per fee services.

❑ **Prodigy:** 445 Hamilton Avenue, White Plains, NY 10601, Tel.
800-PRODIGY or 800-776-3449. Claiming more than 2 million
subscribers, this service also offers several useful career information and networking opportunities through its *Careers BB* and
Classifieds services. Prodigy is especially useful for individuals
conducting a long-distance job search. It includes several major
newspapers and community bulletin boards for surveying different
communities and classified ads.

Most of these commercial online companies offer at least 10 free
hours of connect time to sample their services. If you decide to subscribe,
expect to pay about $10.00 per month, which includes 3-5 free hours of
online time, plus $3.00 for each additional hour. Call their toll-free
numbers for information on their services. In addition to paying monthly
user fees, you will need a computer, modem, and communications
software to interact with these services. Each of these services can advise
you on hardware requirements; they provide the software.

Once you are connected to one or more of these services, chances are
you will be able to access a great deal of employment information useful
to your job search. Most of these services include online classifieds,
career bulletin boards, and discussion forums. Using e-mail, you can
network for information, advice, and referrals. You can explore bulletin
boards for job listings in your particular career field as well as participate
in online discussion groups and seminars, access job search resources,
and receive online counseling. While many services are free, except for
the connect time, others may involve special user or service fees. You'll
quickly discover your online networking opportunities are endless. All
of these services also provide access to the Internet.

THE INTERNET'S WORLD WIDE WEB

If you choose not to use one of the online commercial services, you can
gain direct access to the Internet through an independent service
provider. Within the last year, several new career-related services have
appeared on the Internet's World Wide Web, and several of those which
used to be accessed only through the commercial online services are now

available on the World Wide Web. In fact, this is where much of the online career networking is taking place these days. Some observers predict that the future of commercial online services is now at serious risk since more and more people are gaining direct access to the multitude of new services available on the World Wide Web through independent service providers. This eliminates the need to incur the hourly charges of the commercial online services when using the Internet.

The following organizations now operate databases and career services on the Internet's World Wide Web. Most of them offer a combination of free and fee-based services and products. Some primarily operate as job listing bulletin boards (BBS):

❑ **Adams JobBank Online:** http://www.adamsonline.com. Operated by one of the major publishers of career books, this relatively new online service includes job listings, discussion forums (conferences, workshops, Q&A sessions), specialized career services, and publications.

❑ **America's Job Bank:** http://www.ajb.dni.us. Here's the ultimate "public job bank" that could eventually put some private online entrepreneurs out of business. Operated by the U.S. Department of Labor, this is the closest thing to a comprehensive nationwide computerized job bank. Linked to state employment offices, which daily post thousands of new job listings filed by employers with their offices, individuals should soon be able to explore more than a million job vacancies in both the public and private sectors at any time through this service. Since this is your government at work, this service is free. While the jobs listing cover everything from entry-level to professional and managerial positions, expect to find a disproportionate number of jobs requiring less than a college education listed in this job bank. This service is also available at state employment offices as well as at other locations (look for touch screen kiosks in shopping centers and other public places) which are set up for public use. Useful linkages.

❑ **CareerMosiac:** http://www.careermosaic.com. This job service is appropriate for college students and professionals. Includes hundreds of job listings in a large variety of fields, from high-tech to retail, with useful information on each employer and job. Includes a useful feature whereby college students can communicate directly with employers (e-mail) for information and advice—a good opportunity to do "inside" networking.

❑ **CareerWEB:** http://www.cweb.com. Operated by Landmark Communications (Norfolk, Virginia) which also publishes several newspapers and operates The Weather Channel, The Travel Channel, and InfiNet, this relatively new service is a major recruitment source for hundreds of companies nationwide. Free service for job seekers who can explore hundreds of job listings, many of which are in high-tech fields. Includes company profile pages to learn about a specific company. A quality operation. Also publishes a useful newsletter called *CareerWEB Connections*.

❑ **E-Span:** http://www.espan.com. This full-service online employment resource includes hundreds of job listings in a variety of fields as well as operates a huge database of resumes. Job seekers can send their resumes (e-mail or snail mail) to be included in their database of job listings and search for appropriate job openings through the Interactive Employment Network. Also includes useful career information and resources. If you use commercial online services, E-Span can be accessed through America Online, CompuServe, and GEnie.

❑ **JobTrak:** http://www.jobtrak.com. This organization posts over 500 new job openings each day from companies seeking college students and graduates. Includes company profiles, job hunting tips, and employment information. Good source for entry-level positions, including both full-time and part-time positions, and for researching companies.

❑ **JobWeb:** http://www.jobweb.org. This is the newest and most comprehensive online service targeted for the college scene, following the demise of kiNexus and Connexion. Operated by the National Association of Colleges and Universities (formerly the College Placement Council), this service is designed to do everything: compiles information on employers, including salary surveys; lists job openings; provides job search assistance; and maintains a resume database.

❑ **Online Career Center:** http://www.occ.com/occ. This is the grandaddy of career centers on the Internet. It's basically a resume database and job search service. Individuals send their resume (free if transmitted electronically) which is then included in the database. They also can search for appropriate job openings. Employers pay for using the service. Also available through online commercial services.

❑ **WorkLife:** http://www.worklife.com. Operated by Mainstream Access, which also operates Microsoft Network's Career Center, this is a new service started in March 1996. It offers services for both job seekers and employers in four areas: career, entrepreneurship, human resources, and learning. While some services are free, many specialized services involve fees. For example, employers can use some services to conduct online psychological testing of job candidates. Also includes a career resource center with hundreds of career products, from books to CD-ROMs.

OTHER ELECTRONIC NETWORKS

Commercial online services and career-related World Wide Web sites on the Internet are only the tip of the iceberg when it comes to electronic networking. Numerous professional groups, from the military to health care professionals, have established, or are in the process of creating, their own World Wide Web sites and bulletin boards (BBS). Most of these groups operate discussion forums and networking groups as well as post job openings. If you are just getting started with electronic networking, the groups we've identified thus far should suffice in pointing you in the right direction.

If you know how to use e-mail and surf the Internet, a whole new world of electronic networking opportunities will unfold before your computer screen. You will discover new ways to network your way to job and career success. Indeed, as we write this material, several hundred new networking groups are in the process of developing sites on the Internet. Within the next 12 months a whole new world of networking opportunities will evolve online. Our best advice is this: you should learn how to operate online so you can discover as well as create your own electronic networking opportunities in the future. Your major challenge will be to sort through all the electronic chaos in this new world of electronic networking to get meaningful results! This will not be as easy a task as it may initially appear. Expect to do a lot of electronic communicating that has little or no payoff for your job search.

KEY ELECTRONIC NETWORKING RESOURCES

Several books provide useful information on the new electronic networking era. Among some of the most useful such resources are:

Dixon, Pam and Sylvia Tiersten, *Be Your Own Headhunter: Go Online to Get the Job You Want* (New York: Random House Electronic, 1995)

Glossbrenner, Alfred and Emily, *Finding a Job on the Internet* (New York: McGraw-Hill, 1995)

Godin, Seth, *Point and Click Jobfinder* (Chicago: Dearborn Trade, 1996)

Goodwin, Mary, Deborah Cohn, Donna Spivey, *Net Jobs: How to Use the Internet to Land Your Dream Job* (New York: Michael Wolff & Co. Publishing, 1996)

Gonyea, James C., *Electronic Resumes: Putting Your Resume On-Line* (New York: McGraw-Hill, 1996)

Gonyea, James C., *The On-Line Job Search Companion* (New York: McGraw-Hill, 1995)

Jandt, Fred E. and Mary Nemnick, *Using the Internet in Your Job Search* (Indianapolis, IN: JIST Works, Inc. 1995)

Kennedy, Joyce Lain, *Hook Up, Get Hired* (New York: Wiley & Sons, Inc., 1995)

Kennedy, Joyce Lain and Thomas J. Morrow, *Electronic Job Search Revolution* (New York: Wiley & Sons, Inc., 1995)

Kennedy, Joyce Lain and Thomas J. Morrow, *Electronic Resume Revolution* (New York: Wiley & Sons, Inc. 1995)

Riley, Margaret, Frances Roehm, and Steve Oserman, *The Guide to Internet Job Searching* (Lincolnwood, IL: NTC Publishing, 1996)

Weddle, Peter, *Electronic Resumes for the New Job Market*
(Manassas Park, VA: Impact Publications, 1995)

BEWARE OF THE LAZY WAY
TO JOB SEARCH SUCCESS

While electronic job search services may well be the wave of the future, they will by no means displace the more traditional networking methods identified in this book for finding jobs. These are proven methods used by thousands of successful job seekers. Indeed, there is a danger in thinking that the electronic revolution will offer **the** solution to the inefficiencies and ineffectiveness associated with traditional job search methods. As presently practiced, electronic networking is primarily a high-tech method for disseminating resumes to potential employers and for acquiring information on employers.

The problems with present forms of electronic networking are fourfold. First, most networks are primarily designed for and controlled by employers. Job seekers are only included in the networks for the benefit of employers. Indeed, these electronic networks are mostly funded by employers who have online access to participants' resume data. Job seekers' involvement in these networks is that of passive participant who submits an electronic resume and then waits to hear from employers who may or may not refer to their resume. Not surprising, many job seekers may never hear from employers. From the perspective of the job seeker, such a network is merely a high-tech version of the broadcast resume that is mass mailed to numerous employers—one of the most ineffective resume distribution approaches. However, when it focuses on acquiring information, advice, and referrals, electronic networking may become more useful and effective for job seekers.

Second, electronic resume services give employers limited, albeit important, information on candidates. These services are primarily efficient resume screening techniques that communicate little information about the individual beyond traditional resume categories. Employers still need to screen candidates on other criteria, especially in face-to-face settings, which enable them to assess a candidate's personal chemistry. Such information is best communicated through the networking process we identified in previous chapters.

Third, the major sponsors and participants—large Fortune 1000 companies—in the electronic resume banks are not the ones that do most of the hiring. These are the same companies that have been shedding jobs—nearly 5 million in the past eight years—rather than adding them to the job market. The companies that do the most hiring and thus add the most jobs to the workforce—small companies with fewer than 500 employees—are not major participants in the electronic resume banks. Therefore, you are well advised to target your job search toward the companies that generate the most jobs. You do so by using the major networking techniques outlined earlier in this book.

Fourth, the quality of information, advice, and referrals gained from electronic networking may be very poor or nearly useless because of the types of individuals participating in such relatively anonymous networks. You may, for example, be communicating with a kid, someone who is unemployed, people with little or no experience, or even a scam artist or a sociopath! Busy employers and employment experts—those who can really make a difference when you are engaged in quality networking—don't have the luxury of spending time online networking with strangers. If they did, they might soon be out of a job for engaging in what are ostensibly nonproductive activities.

So where does this all lead in the larger scheme of networking and the job search? We recommend that you include electronic networking in your overall repertoire of networking methods and job search activities. But put this electronic networking alternative in its proper perspective—an efficient way to broadcast your qualifications to employers through an electronic resume as well as acquire potentially useful information about jobs, employers, and job search methods. Above all, avoid paying for questionable online employment services; check out an organization's performance before you send money. Don't approach electronic networking as the easy way to job search success; there's nothing magical about disseminating resumes electronically nor communicating with strangers by e-mail. Sending a $50 membership fee and a resume to one of these firms ensures you nothing other than a presence in an electronic resume bank. What happens next—whether or not you are contacted by employers—depends on an unpredictable mix of factors, such as the number and quality of employer members in the system, employer hiring needs at any specific time, and the quality of your electronic resume, especially your choice of resume language.

Finding a job still remains hard work. While it does take place within a chaotic arena—the job market—it does not involve a random communication process. Finding a job requires a great deal of purposeful networking initiative on your part. Above all, you must take action aimed at specific organizations and employers on a daily basis. And that's what our networking techniques in previous chapters are all about.

10

RESOURCES FOR SUCCESSFUL JOB NETWORKING

S uccessful networking also involves knowing which resources are the most useful for conducting a job search. While you chose this book as one of your resources, you should also discover many other resources that complement as well as extend this book into other critical job search steps.

Throughout this book we have mentioned several resources we feel will assist you with your job search and networking activities. Let's now turn to what we consider to be some of the best resources available for further expanding your job search beyond this book. Our goal is to bring some coherence and organization to this literature to assist you in identifying additional resources that might be useful to you in your job search. Since many of these resources cannot be found in local bookstores or libraries, you may need to order them directly from the publishers. For your convenience, many of these books are available through Impact Publications by completing the order form at the end of this book.

We mainly deal with books here, because they are the least expensive and most easily accessible resources in bookstores and libraries. However, more and more computer software programs and CD-ROMs are now available to assist you with four stages in your job search: self-assessment, research, resume writing, and employer contacts. Many career planning centers and some libraries and computer stores offer these resources. We include several of the most useful programs in this chapter.

CHOOSE WHAT'S BEST FOR YOU

During the past 20 years hundreds of self-help books have been written on how to find a job and advance one's career. Each year dozens of additional volumes are published to inform as well as enlighten a growing audience of individuals concerned with conducting a proper job search.

You may be initially overwhelmed with the sheer volume of the career planning and job search literature available to help individuals find jobs and change careers. Once you examine a few books you will quickly learn that this literature is designed to be **used**. The books are not designed to describe or explain reality, develop a theory, nor predict the future.

Most career planning and job search books are designed to advance self-help strategies based upon the particular ideas or experiences of individual writers. They expound a **set of beliefs**—more or less logical and based on both experience and faith. Like other how-to literature on achieving success, you must first **believe** in these books before you can make them work for you. These books must be judged on the basis of faith and usefulness.

Given the nature of this literature, your best approach is to pick and choose which books are more or less useful for you. There is nothing magical about these books. At best, they may challenge your preconceptions; present alternative beliefs which you may or may not find acceptable; provide you with some directions; and help motivate you to implement an effective job search. They will not get you a job.

The level of redundancy in this literature may disturb many readers. More so than in many other fields, career planning writers tend to quote each other or rely on the perspectives of a few key writers in restating the same approaches in a different form. As a result, many individuals confuse the high level of redundancy as repeated evidence of career and job "facts."

CONVENTIONAL VERSUS ELECTRONIC JOB SEARCHES

Beginning in 1994, a significant shift in emphasis began with the increasing appearance of books on how to conduct an electronic job search via resume databases, commercial online services, and the Internet. A whole new body of job search literature, represented by such books as Joyce Lain Kennedy's *Electronic Job Search Revolution* and *Hook Up Get Hired*, Pam Dixon's *Be Your Own Headhunter Online*, and James Gonyea's *The On-Line Job Search Companion*, emerged on how to conduct an electronic job search. Unfortunately, most of these new books become obsolete the day they come off press because of the rapid changes taking place in the electronic arena. These books merely reflected changes taking place in the work world, changes which had not yet been addressed in most job search literature.

Not surprising, most job search literature published before 1994 now seems dated because it does not address the new issue of conducting an electronic job search. And anything produced after 1995 which does not address the issue of the electronic job search in some form seems dated, raising questions about its usefulness for job seekers.

WHAT YOU GET

We have examined most of the career planning and job search literature with a view toward identifying the best of the lot. We've judged the literature in terms of its degree of accuracy, realism, comprehensiveness, and usefulness. In doing so, we have found three major types of books which use different approaches to getting a job:

- Books designed to teach individuals key job search **process and strategy skills**; these books emphasize "how" questions. Many of them now fall into two distinct categories: interpersonal versus electronic strategies.

- Books designed to outline various **employment fields**; these books emphasize "what" and "where" questions.

- Books designed to address key career issues for **special groups**; these books emphasize "what" and "how" questions.

A growing number of comprehensive job search books attempt to apply the process and strategy skills to different employment fields and special groups.

PROCESS AND STRATEGY SKILLS

The first type of career planning and job search literature concentrates primarily on developing **process and strategy skills**. Most of these books tell you **how** to develop an effective job search regardless of your particular employment field or your specialized needs. They seldom address substantive **what** and **where** questions central to finding any job. You are left to answer these questions on your own or by using other resources which focus on what jobs are available and where to find them.

There are few surprises in this literature since most of the books follow a similar pattern in approaching the subject. The major difference is that the books are more or less readable. In addition, many of these books now fall into two distinctive, and at times competing, categories: interpersonal versus electronic job search methods. Most of the interpersonal process books are preoccupied with "getting in touch with yourself" by emphasizing the need to "know what you want to do today, tomorrow, and the rest of your life." The electronic job search methods books tend to focus on the mechanics of how to "surf the Net" by acquiring new electronic networking skills.

Some of the interpersonal process literature is rightly referred to as "touchy-feely" because of its concern with trying to get to know yourself —the basis for self-assessment. A mainstay of psychologists, counselors, and activity-oriented trainers, this type of positive, up-beat literature is at best designed to reorient your life around (1) identifying what is right about yourself (your strengths), and (2) setting goals based upon an understanding of your past and present in the hope you will do better in the future (your objectives).

The electronic job search literature tends to be preoccupied with developing technical expertise for finding job listings, broadcasting resumes, and conducting research online; it does not deal with key self-assessment and interpersonal communication issues.

Both types of literature still deal with the key challenge facing job seekers—how to best communicate their qualifications to employers.

The real strengths of this process literature lie in orienting your thinking along new lines, providing you with some baseline information on your strengths and goals, providing you with positive motivation for developing and implementing an effective job search strategy, and outlining useful how-to strategies and techniques for penetrating the job market. If you're looking for specifics, such as learning what the jobs are and where you can find them, this literature may disappoint you with its vagueness.

Placed within our career planning framework in Chapter 3, much of this process and strategy literature falls into the initial two steps of our career planning process: self-assessment and objective setting. Examples of career planning literature using this approach are the popular books written by Bolles, Miller and Mattson, Crystal, Sher, and Tieger: *Where Do I Go From Here With My Life?*, *The Three Boxes of Life*, *The Truth About You*, *Do What You Are*, *I Could Do Anything If Only I Knew What It Was*, and *Wishcraft*. Other books, such as Bolles' *The New Quick Job Hunting Map*, Dahl and Sykes' *Charting Your Goals*, the Gales' *Discover What You're Best At*, Yeager's *CareerMap*, Chapman's *Be True to Your Future*, and Sturman's *Career Discovery Project*, provide useful exercises for identifying goals and assessing abilities and skills. The Krannichs' *Discover the Best Jobs For You!* synthesizes much of this self-assessment literature. You should read some of these books if you lack a clear understanding of who you are, what you want to do, and where you are going. They will help you get in touch with yourself before you get in touch with employers!

Several books, similar to this one, focus on additional steps in the career planning and job search processes, such as doing research, writing resumes and letters, networking, interviewing, and negotiating salaries. While also emphasizing process and strategy, these are more comprehensive books than the others. Some books include all of the job search steps whereas others concentrate on one or two. Examples of the most comprehensive such books include those written by Krannich, Bolles, Yate, Lucht, Wegmann and Chapman, MacDonald, Lathrop,

Messmer, Jackson, Figler, and Studner: *Change Your Job Change Your Life*, *What Color Is Your Parachute?*, *Knock 'Em Dead*, *Rites of Passage at $100,000+*, *The Right Place At the Right Time*, *Who's Hiring Who*, *Job Hunting For Dummies*, *The Complete Job Search Handbook*, *Guerrilla Tactics In the New Job Market*, *The Complete Job Finder's Guide For the 90's*, and *Super Job Search*.

At the same time, several new books by Kennedy, Dixon, Gonyea, Glossbrenner, Godin, Jandt, Nemnick, and Wolfe now focus on conducting an electronic job search, with most such books increasingly concentrating on using the Internet for networking, identifying job openings, and broadcasting resumes: *Electronic Job Search Revolution*, *Net Jobs*, *Be Your Own Headhunter Online*, *The On-Line Job Search Companion*, *Finding a Job on the Internet*, *Point and Click Jobfinder*, *Using the Internet in Your Job Search*, and *Hook Up, Get Hired*.

Several new multi-media products now integrate books with videos. One of the best and most comprehensive is InfoBusiness' *The Ultimate Job Source CD-ROM*. Others include DataTech's *You're Hired*, WinWay's *Win-Way Resume 3.0*, and Individual Software's *Resume-Maker*.

You will find hundreds of books that focus on the **research stage** of the job search. Most of these books are geographic, field, or organizational directories or job banks which list names and addresses of potential employers. Examples include the Adams Media's *Job Bank Series* on 20 major cities and metropolitan areas and *Job Bank Guide to Employment Services*, Surrey Book's *How to Get a Job In...* series on ten cities, Career Communications' *Job Hotlines*, Kennedy Publication's *Directory of Executive Recruiters*, Wright's *American Almanac of Jobs and Salaries*, Schwartz's and Brechner's *The Career Finder, Hoover's Handbook of American Business*, Levering's *100 Best Companies to Work For in America*, and Dun and Bradstreet's *The Career Guide: Dun's Employment Opportunity Directory*. Job search approaches relating to much of this literature are in sharp contrast to approaches of the standard career planning literature. Directories, for example, should be used to gather information—names, addresses, and phone numbers—to be used in targeting one's networking activities rather than as sources for shotgunning resumes and letters.

Numerous books are written on other key job search steps—especially resume and letter writing and job interviews. The **resume and letter writing** books fall into three major categories:

- Books designed to walk you through the process of developing a resume based upon a thorough understanding of each step in the job search process. Examples include Krannich's and Banis' *High Impact Resumes and Letters*, Jackson's *The Perfect Resume*, Fry's *Your First Resume*, Swanson's *The Resume Solution*, and Good's *Does Your Resume Wear Blue Jeans?*

- Books primarily presenting examples of resumes and letters. Examples of such books are numerous—most resume and letter writing books you will find in libraries and bookstores fall in this category. One of the best such books is Parker's *The Resume Catalog*. Others include Parker's *The Damn Good Resume Guide*, *The Resume Pro*, *Ready-to-Go Resumes*, and *Blue Collar and Beyond*; Noble's *Gallery of Best Resumes*; Career Press' *Resumes Resumes Resumes*; Fein's *Cover Letters, Cover Letters, Cover Letters*; Frank's *200 Letters For Job Hunters*; Beatty's *The Perfect Cover Letter* and *175 High-Impact Cover Letters*; Yate's *Resumes That Knock 'Em Dead* and *Cover Letters That Knock 'Em Dead*; and the Krannichs' *Dynamite Resumes* and *Job Search Letters That Get Results*.

- Books focusing solely on developing an electronic resume to be used with electronic databases and online services. Examples of such books include Kennedy's *Electronic Resume Revolution*, Weddle's *Electronic Resumes For the New Job Market*, Gonyea's *Electronic Resumes*, and Wright's *Resumes For People Who Hate to Write Resumes*.

The first type of resume and letter writing book urges the user to develop resumes and letters that represent the "unique you" in relation to specific positions and employers. Incorporating much of the approach used in this book, they emphasize the importance of finding a job that is right for you rather than try to adjust your skills and experience to fit into a job that may be inappropriate for you. These books are based upon a particular approach to finding a job as outlined in several of the comprehensive career planning and job search books.

The second type of resume and letter writing book lacks a clear approach other than an implied suggestion that readers should creatively plagiarize the examples. In other words, good resumes and letters are produced by osmosis!

The third type of resume book deals with the special case of electronic resumes. These books combine the writing process with examples of electronic resumes. Most also address the issue of how to distribute these resumes electronically.

Several books address **networking**. While many job search books include a short section on networking—discuss the importance of networking and give a few examples of networks and networking—the present book—*Dynamite Networking For Dynamite Jobs*—is the only book to focus solely on the role of networking in the job search process as well as incorporate interpersonal, telephone, and electronic networking. Boe and Young's *Is Your "Net" Working* looks at how to build contacts for career development. Other books, such as Baber and Waymon's *Great Connections*, Erdman and Sullivan's *Network Your Way to Success,* Giovagnoli's *Make Your Connections Count!*, Venda Raye-Johnson's *Effective Networking,* and Roane's *How to Work a Room* and *The Secrets of Savvy Networking*, approach networking from the perspective of small talk in business and social settings. Vilas' *Power Networking* synthesizes several approaches to networking as a set of networking principles. Baker's *Networking Smart* is one of the most thorough treatments of the networking phenomenon. National Business Employment Weekly's *Networking*, Garnas' *How to Use People and Get What You Want*, and Lowstuter's and Robertson's *Network Your Way to Your Next Job...Fast* focus on interpersonal networking relevant to the job search. Dixon's and Tiersten's *Be Your Own Headhunter Online* includes a separate chapter devoted solely to electronic networking in the job search. The ultimate CD-ROM for networking is probably *Select Phone CD-ROM* which includes 80 million residential and 15 million business names, addresses, and phone numbers.

You will also find several **job interview** books designed for both interviewees and interviewers. Most of these books examine each step in the interview process—from preparation to negotiating salary. Some of these books, such as Fein's *101 Dynamite Questions to Ask at Your Interview*, Fry's *101 Great Answers to the Toughest Interview Questions*, Allen's *The Complete Q & A Job Interview Book,* and the Krannichs' *Dynamite Answers to Interview Questions* focus primarily on questions and answers. Other books, such as the Krannichs' *Interview For Success* and Medley's *Sweaty Palms* are more comprehensive, including interview settings, types of interviews, and nonverbal communication along with a discussion of appropriate questions and answers.

While most comprehensive job search and interview books include a section on salary negotiations, a few books have been written on this subject. However, some of these books are now out of print, but they may be available in your local library. Examples include the Krannichs' *Dynamite Salary Negotiations*, Kennedy's *Salary Strategies*, Chastain's *Winning the Salary Game*, and Chapman's *How to Make $1000 a Minute*. Much of the general literature on negotiation tactics is relevant to this topic.

SPECIFIC EMPLOYMENT FIELDS

A second type of career and job search literature focuses primarily on specific employment fields. These books come in many forms. Some are designed to give the reader a general overview of what type of work is involved in each field. Other books include educational training and job search strategies appropriate for entry into each field. And still others are annotated listings of job and career titles—the most comprehensive being the Department of Labor's *Occupational Outlook Handbook* and *The Dictionary of Occupational Titles*.

The majority of books on employment fields are designed for individuals who are considering a particular employment field rather than for individuals wishing to advance within a field. Some books identify the best jobs at present and for the future, such as Krannichs' *The Best Jobs For the 1990s and Into the 21st Century*, Petras' *Jobs 1996* (annual), Kleiman's *The 100 Best Jobs For the 1990s and Beyond*, and Krantz's *Jobs Rated Almanac*. Other books are general introductions designed to answer important "what," "where," and "how" questions for high school and college students. They provide little useful information for older and more experienced professionals. Examples of such books include the 160+ volumes in National Textbook's *Opportunities in... Series* with such titles as *Opportunities in Architecture, Opportunities in Office Occupations, Opportunities in Public Relations, Opportunities in Forestry,* and *Opportunities in Travel Careers*. Visible Ink Press publishes 20 career directories with such titles as *Education Career Directory, Newspapers Career Directory,* and *Business and Finance Career Directory*. Impact Publications specializes in books in fields of government, international, and travel with such titles as *Find a Federal Job Fast, Directory of Federal Jobs and Employers, Almanac of International Jobs and Careers, Jobs Worldwide,* and *Jobs For People Who Love Travel*. More and more books are being produced on specific employment fields, especially for computer, business, health care, government, international, communication, media, and travel specialists.

SPECIALIZED CAREER GROUPS

A final set of career planning and job search books has emerged during the past few years. These books are designed for specific groups of job seekers who supposedly need specialized assistance not found in most general job search process and employment field books. The most common such books focus on women, minorities, the handicapped, immigrants, public employees, military personnel, educators, mobile spouses, college graduates, children, and teenagers.

Many of these books represent a new type of career planning book that has emerged during the past few years and will most likely continue in the foreseeable future. Several books deal with both **process** and **substance**. They link the substantive "what" and "where" concerns of specific employment fields to "how" processes appropriately outlined for each field.

Take, for example, the field of advertising. Several books, such as Caffrey's *So You Want to Be in Advertising,* Mogal's *Making It in the Media Professions,* and Bradley's *The Advertising Career Directory*, outline the jobs available in the field of advertising (*what questions*), where you should look for vacancies (*where questions*), and the best strategies for finding a job, including resumes, letters, and interview questions appropriate for the advertising field (*how questions*).

These specialized career books finally identify how general job search strategies must be adapted and modified to respond to the employment needs of different types of individuals as well as to the employment cultures found in different fields. Some of the most popular such books include *The Minority Career Handbook, Job Strategies For People With Disabilities, Getting a Job in the United States, The Complete Guide to Public Employment, The Complete Guide to International Jobs and Careers, The Educator's Guide to Alternative Jobs and Careers, The New Relocating Spouse's Guide to Employment, Retiring From the Military, Liberal Arts Jobs,* and *Summer Opportunities For Kids and Teenagers*.

In the coming decade we can expect to see more career planning books produced along these combined process, field, and group lines. While general career planning books focusing only on process and strategy will continue to proliferate, with more and more attention given to the "electronic job search revolution," the real excitement in this field will be centered around the continuing development of resources which link process to specific employment fields and specialized groups. If, for example, you are in the fields of real estate or robotics, you should be able to find books outlining what the jobs are, where to find them, and how to get them. Such books will most likely be written by seasoned professionals in particular fields and representing specialized groups rather than by career planning professionals who are primarily trained in process skills. Such books will meet a growing need for information from individuals who have a solid understanding of how to get a job based on familiarity with the "ins" and "outs" of each field.

The following bibliography includes some of the best career planning resources available today. Consistent with the structure of this book and our discussion of career planning and job search literature, we have organized the bibliography according to process, field, and group categories. We've integrated both conventional and electronic resources into the same categories rather than treat them separately.

BIBLIOGRAPHY

Job Search Strategies and Tactics

Adams Media, *Adams Jobs Almanac 1996* (Holbrook, MA: Adams Media, annual)

Bolles, Richard N., *What Color Is Your Parachute?* (Berkeley, CA: Ten Speed Press, annual)

Dixon, Pam and Sylvia Tiersten, *Be Your Own Headhunter Online* (New York: Random House, 1995)

Doric Marc, *The Complete Idiot's Guide to Getting the Job You Want* (New York: Alpha Books, 1995)

Elderkin, Kenneth, *How to Get Interviews From Classified Job Ads* (Manassas Park, VA: Impact Publications, 1993)

Figler, Howard E., *The Complete Job Search Handbook* (New York: Holt, Rinehart, and Winston, 1988)

Glossbrenner, Alfred and Emily, *Finding a Job On the Internet* (New York: McGraw-Hill, 1995)

Godin, Seth, *Point and Click Jobfinder* (Chicago, IL: Dearborn Financial Publishing, 1996)

Gonyea, James C., *The On-Line Job Search Companion* (New York: McGraw Hill, 1995)

Goodwin, Mary, Deborah Cohn, Donna Spivey, *Net Jobs: How to Use the Internet to Land Your Dream Job* (New York: Michael Wolff & Co. Publishing, 1996)

Jackson, Tom, *Guerrilla Tactics in the New Job Market* (New York: Bantam, 1991)

Kennedy, Joyce Lain and Darryl Laramore, *The Joyce Lain Kennedy's Career Book* (Lincolnwood, IL: NTC Publishing, 1996)

Kennedy, Joyce Lain and Thomas J. Morrow, *Electronic Job Search Revolution* (New York: Wiley, 1995)

Kennedy, Joyce Lain, *Hook Up, Get Hired* (New York: Wiley, 1995)

Krannich, Ronald L., *Change Your Job, Change Your Life* (Manassas Park, VA: Impact Publications, 1995)

Lathrop, Richard, *Who's Hiring Who* (Berkeley, CA: Ten Speed Press, 1989)

Lucht, John, *Rites of Passage at $100,000+* (New York: Henry Holt, 1993)

McDonald, Scott A., *The Complete Job Finder's Guide For the 90's* (Manassas Park, VA: Impact Publications, 1993)

Messmer, Max, *Job Hunting For Dummies* (Foster City, CA: IDG Books Worldwide, 1995)

Siegel, Barbara L. and Robert S., *The Five Secrets to Finding a Job: A Story of Success* (Manassas Park, VA: Impact Publications, 1994)

Riley, Margaret, Frances Roehm, and Steve Oserman, *The Guide to Internet Job Searching* (Lincolnwood, IL: NTC Publishing, 1996)

Studner, Peter K., *Super Job Search* (Los Angeles, CA: Jamenair Ltd., 1995)

Yate, Martin, *Knock 'Em Dead 1996* (Holbrook, MA: Adams Media, annual)

Wegmann, Robert and Robert Chapman, *The Right Place At the Right Time* (Berkeley, CA: Ten Speed Press, 1990)

Skills Identification, Testing, and Self-Assessment

Bolles, Richard N., *The New Quick Job Hunting Map* (Berkeley, CA: Ten Speed Press, 1990)

Bolles, Richard N., *The Three Boxes of Life* (Berkeley, CA: Ten Speed Press, 1981)

Crystal, John C. and Richard N. Bolles, *Where Do I Go From Here With My Life?* (Berkeley, CA: Ten Speed Press, 1979)

Dahl, Dan and Randolph Sykes, *Charting Your Goals* (New York: Harper and Row, 1988)

Gale, Barry and Linda Gale, *Discover What You're Best At* (New York: Simon & Schuster, 1990)

Holland, John L., *Making Vocational Choices* (Englewood Cliffs, NJ: Prentice-Hall, 1985)

Krannich, Ronald L. and Caryl Rae Krannich, *Discover the Best Jobs For You!* (Manassas Park, VA: Impact Publications, 1993)

Miller, Arthur F. and Ralph T. Mattson, *The Truth About You: Discover What You Should Be Doing With Your Life* (Berkeley, CA: Ten Speed Press, 1989)

Sher, Barbara and Barbara Smith, *I Could Do Anything If I Only Knew What It Was* (New York: Delacorte Press, 1994)

Sher, Barbara and Annie Gottlieb, *Wishcraft: How To Get What You Really Want* (New York: Ballantine, 1986)

Sturman, Gerald M., *The Career Discover Project* (New York: Bantam, 1993)

Tieger, Paul and Barbara Barron-Tieger, *Do What You Are* (New York: Little, Brown, 1995)

Research On Cities, Fields, and Organizations

Adams Media, *The Job Bank Series: Atlanta, Boston, Chicago, Dallas/Fort Worth, Denver, Detroit, Florida, Houston, Los Angeles, Minneapolis, New York, Ohio, Philadelphia, Phoenix, San Francisco, Seattle, St. Louis, Washington, DC* (Holbrook, MA: Adams Media, annuals)

Adams Media (eds.), *The National Job Bank* (Holbrook, MA: Adams Media, annual)

Camden, Bishop, Schwartz, Greene, Fleming-Holland, *"How To Get a Job in..." Insider's City Guides: Atlanta, Boston, Chicago, Dallas/Ft. Worth, Houston, New York, San Francisco, Seattle/Portland, Southern California, Washington, DC* (Chicago, IL: Surrey Books, biannuals)

Diefenbach, Greg and Phil Giordano, *Jobs in Washington, DC* (Manassas Park, VA: Impact Publications, 1992)

Harkavy, Michael, *101 Careers* (New York: Wiley, 1994)

Hoover, Gary, Alta Campbell, and Patrick J. Spain, *Hoover's Handbook of American Business* and *Hoover's Handbook of World Business* (Austin, TX: The Reference Press, annual)

Hopke, William (ed.), *Encyclopedia of Careers and Vocational Guidance* (Chicago, IL: J. G. Ferguson, 1993)

Kleiman, Carol, *The 100 Best Jobs For the 1990s and Beyond* (Chicago, IL: Dearborn Trade, 1992)

Krannich, Ronald L. and Caryl Rae Krannich, *Best Jobs For the 1990s and Into the 21st Century* (Manassas Park, VA: Impact Publications, 1995)

Krantz, Les, *The Jobs Rated Almanac* (New York: Wiley, 1995)

Lauber, Daniel, *The Professional's Private Sector Job Finder* (River Forest, IL: Planning/Communication, 1994).

Morgan, Bradley J. (ed.), *The Career Directory Series: Advertising, Book Publishing, Business and Finance, Healthcare, Magazine Publishing, Marketing and Sales, Newspaper Publishing, Public Relations, Radio and Television, Travel and Hospitality* (Detroit, MI: Gale Research, 1993-1995)

Norback, Craig T., *Careers Encyclopedia* (Lincolnwood, IL: National Textbook, 1992)

Petras, Ross and Kathryn, *Jobs 1996* (New York: Simon & Schuster, annual)

U.S. Department of Labor, *Dictionary of Occupational Titles* (Washington, DC: U.S. Department of Labor, 1991)

U.S. Department of Labor, *The Occupational Outlook Handbook* (Washington, DC: U.S. Department of Labor, 1996, biannual)

Wright, John W., *The American Almanac of Jobs and Salaries* (New York: Avon, 1993)

Relocation Decisions

Bastress, Frances, *The New Relocating Spouse's Guide to Employment* (Manassas Park, VA: Impact Publications, 1993)

Omnigraphics, Inc. (ed.), *Moving and Relocation Sourcebook* (Detroit, MI: Omnigraphics, Inc., 1993)

Resumes and Letters

Beatty, Richard H., *175 High-Impact Cover Letters* (New York: Wiley, 1992)

Beatty, Richard H., *The Perfect Cover Letter* (New York: Wiley, 1989)

Frank, William S., *200 Letters For Job Hunters* (Berkeley, CA: Ten Speed Press, 1994)

Fry, Ronald W., *Your First Resume* (Hawthorne, NJ: Career Press, 1994)

Gonyea, Jams C., *Electronic Resumes: A Complete Guide to Putting Your Resume On-Line* (New York: McGraw-Hill, 1996)

Good, C. Edward, *Resumes For Re-Entry* (Manassas Park, VA: Impact Publications, 1993)

Jackson, Tom, *The Perfect Resume* (New York: Doubleday, 1993)

Kennedy, Joyce Lain and Thomas J. Morrow, *Electronic Resume Revolution* (New York: Wiley, 1995)

Krannich, Ronald L. and Caryl Rae Krannich, *Dynamite Cover Letters* (Manassas Park, VA: Impact Publications, 1996)

Krannich, Ronald L. and Caryl Rae Krannich, *Dynamite Resumes* (Manassas Park, VA: Impact Publications, 1996)

Krannich, Ronald L. and William J. Banis, *High Impact Resumes and Letters* (Manassas Park, VA: Impact Publications, 1995)

Krannich, Ronald L. and Caryl Rae Krannich, *Job Search Letters That Get Results: 201 Great Examples* (Manassas Park, VA: Impact Publications, 1995)

Noble, David F., *Gallery of Best Resumes* (Indianapolis, IN: JIST Works, 1994)

Parker, Yana, *Blue Collar and Beyond* (Berkeley, NY: Ten Speed Press, 1994)

Parker, Yana, *The Damn Good Resume Guide* (Berkeley, NY: Ten Speed Press, 1996)

Parker, Yana, *Ready-to-Go Resumes* (Berkeley, NY: Ten Speed Press, 1994)

Parker, Yana, *The Resume Catalog* (Berkeley, NY: Ten Speed Press, 1988)

Parker, Yana, *The Resume Pro* (Berkeley, NY: Ten Speed Press, 1992)

Swanson, David, *The Resume Solution* (Indianapolis, IN: JIST Works, 1994)

Weddle, Peter, *Electronic Resumes For the New Job Market* (Manassas Park, VA: Impact Publications, 1995)

Wright, Jack W., *Resumes For People Who Hate to Write Resumes* (Livermore, CA: Shastar Press, 1994)

Yate, Martin, *Cover Letters That Knock 'Em Dead* (Holbrook, MA: Adams Media, annual)

Yate, Martin, *Resumes That Knock 'Em Dead* (Holbrook, MA: Adams Media, annual)

Networking

Baber, Anne and Lynne Waymon, *Great Connections: Small Talk and Networking For Businesspeople* (Manassas Park, VA: Impact Publications, 1991)

Baker, Wayne E., *Networking Smart: How to Build Relationships For Personal and Organizational Success* (New York: McGraw-Hill, 1994)

Boe, Anne and Bettie B. Youngs, *Is Your "Net" Working?* (New York: Wiley, 1989)

Garnas, Les, *How to Use People and Get What You Want—and Still Be a Nice Guy!* (Princeton, NJ: Peterson's, 1994)

Giovagnoli, Melissa, *Make Your Connections Count!* (Chicago, IL: Dearborn Financial Publishing, 1995).

Krannich, Ronald L. and Caryl Rae Krannich, *Dynamite Networking For Dynamite Jobs* (Manassas Park, VA: Impact Publications, 1996)

Lowstuter, Clyde C. And David P. Robertson, *Network Your Way to Your Next Job...Fast* (New York: McGraw-Hill, 1995)

Raye-Johnson, Venda, *Effective Networking* (Palo Alto, CA: Crisp Publications, 1990)

Roane, Susan, *How to Work a Room* (New York: Warner Books, 1989)

Roane, Susan, *The Secrets of Savvy Networking* (New York: Warner Books, 1993)

Vilas, Donna and Sandy, *Power Networking* (Austin, TX: MountainHarbour Publications, 1992)

Dress, Image, Etiquette

Gray, Jr., James, *The Winning Image* (New York: Amacom, 1993)

Dunckel, Jacqueline, *Business Etiquette* (Bellingham, WA: Self-Counsel Press, 1992)

Karpinski, Kenneth J., *Red Socks Don't Work: Messages From the Real World About Men's Clothing* (Manassas Park, VA: Impact Publications, 1994)

Nicholson, JoAnna, *110 Mistakes Working Women Make and How to Avoid Them: Dressing Smart in the '90s* (Manassas Park, VA: Impact Publications, 1995)

Interviews and Salary Negotiations

Beatty, R. H., *The Five Minute Interview* (New York: Wiley, 1986)

Chapman, Jack, *How to Make $1000 A Minute: Negotiating Salaries and Raises* (Berkeley, CA: Ten Speed Press, 1987)

Fein, Richard, *101 Dynamite Questions to Ask At Your Job Interview* (Manassas Park, VA: Impact Publications, 1996)

Fein, Richard, *101 Dynamite Ways to Ace Your Job Interview* (Manassas Park, VA: Impact Publications, 1996)

Fry, Ron, *101 Great Answers to the Toughest Interview Questions* (Hawthorne, NJ: Career Press, 1995)

Krannich, Caryl Rae and Ronald L. Krannich, *Dynamite Answers to Interview Questions: No More Sweaty Palms!* (Manassas Park, VA: Impact Publications, 1994)

Krannich, Ronald L. and Caryl Rae Krannich, *Dynamite Salary Negotiations* (Manassas Park, VA: Impact Publications, 1994)

Krannich, Ronald L. and Caryl Rae Krannich, *Dynamite Tele-Search* (Manassas Park, VA: Impact Publications, 1995)

Krannich, Caryl Rae and Ronald L. Krannich, *Interview For Success* (Manassas Park, VA: Impact Publications, 1995)

Medley, H. Anthony, *Sweaty Palms* (Berkeley, CA: Ten Speed Press, 1991)

Ryan, Robin, *60 Seconds and You're Hired!* (Manassas Park, VA: Impact Publications, 1995)

Government and Nonprofit Careers

Jankowski, Katherine, *The Job Seeker's Guide to Socially Responsible Companies* (Detroit, MI: Visible Ink Press, 1995)

Krannich, Ronald L. and Caryl Rae Krannich, *The Directory of Federal Jobs and Employers* (Manassas Park, VA: Impact Publications, 1996)

Krannich, Ronald L. and Caryl Rae Krannich, *The Complete Guide to Public Employment* (Manassas Park, VA: Impact Publications, 1995)

Krannich, Ronald L. and Caryl Rae Krannich, *Find a Federal Job Fast!* (Manassas Park, VA: Impact Publications, 1995)

Krannich, Ronald L. and Caryl Rae Krannich, *Jobs and Careers With Nonprofit Organizations* (Manassas Park, VA: Impact Publications, 1995)

Lauber, Daniel, *The Government Job Finder* (River Forest, IL: Planning/Communications, 1994)

Lauber, Daniel, *The Nonprofits' Job Finder* (River Forest, IL: Planning/Communications, 1994)

Smith, Russ, *Federal Applications That Get Results* (Manassas Park, VA: Impact Publications, 1995)

International and Overseas Jobs

Forbes, Moira, *Jobs in Russia and the Newly Independent States* (Manassas Park, VA: Impact Publications, 1994)

Foreign Policy Association (ed.), *Guide to Careers in World Affairs* (Manassas Park, VA: Impact Publications, 1993)

Kocher, Eric, *International Jobs* (Reading, MA: Addison-Wesley, 1994)

Krannich, Ronald L. and Caryl Rae Krannich, *The Almanac of International Jobs and Careers* (Manassas Park, VA: Impact Publications, 1994)

Krannich, Ronald L. and Caryl Rae Krannich, *The Complete Guide to International Jobs and Careers* (Manassas Park, VA: Impact Publications, 1992)

Krannich, Ronald L. and Caryl Rae Krannich, *Jobs For People Who Love Travel* (Manassas Park, VA: Impact Publications, 1995)

Lay, David and Benedict A. Leerburger, *Jobs Worldwide* (Manassas Park, VA: Impact Publications, 1996)

Sanborn, Robert, *How to Get a Job in Europe* (Chicago, IL: Surrey Books, 1993)

Sanborn, Robert, *How to Get a Job in the Pacific Rim* (Chicago, IL: Surrey Books, 1992)

Military

Henderson, David G., *Job Search: Marketing Your Military Experience in the 1990s* (Harrisburg, PA: Stackpole Books, 1994)

Jacobsen, Kenneth C., *Retiring From the Military* (Annapolis, MD: Naval Institute Press, 1994)

Nyman, Keith O., *Re-Entry: Turning Military Experience Into Civilian Success* (Harrisonburg, PA: Stackpole Books, 1990)

Savino, Carl and Ronald L. Krannich, *From Air Force Blue to Corporate Gray* (Manassas Park, VA: Impact Publications, 1996)

Savino, Carl and Ronald L. Krannich, *From Army Green to Corporate Gray* (Manassas Park, VA: Impact Publications, 1994)

Savino, Carl and Ronald L. Krannich, *From Navy Blue to Corporate Gray* (Manassas Park, VA: Impact Publications, 1995)

Minorities and Disabled

Johnson, Willis L. (ed.), *The Big Book of Minority Opportunities* (Garrett Park, MD: Garrett Park Press, 1995)

Kastre, Michael, Alfred G. Edwards, and Nydia Rodriguez Kastre, *The Minority Career Guide* (Princeton, NJ: Peterson's, 1993)

Rivera, Miquela, *The Minority Career Book* (Holbrook, MA: Adams Media, 1991)

Witt, Melanie Astaire, *Job Strategies For People With Disabilities* (Princeton, NJ: Peterson's, 1992)

Computer Software Programs

Cambridge Career Counseling System (Charleston, WV: Cambridge Career Products)

EZ-DOT (Spokane, WA: Job Quest)

INSTANT™ Job Search Letters (Englewood, CO: CareerLab)

JOBHUNT™ (Greenville, NC: Scope International)

Quick & Easy Federal Application Kit (Harrisburg, PA: Data Tech)

Resumemaker™ With Career Planner (Los Angeles, CA: Individual Software)

You're Hired (Harrisburg, PA: Data Tech)

CD-ROM Programs

JobSearch in Action (Orem, UT: InfoBusiness)

The Multimedia Career Center (Charleston, WV: Cambridge Career Products)

Select Phone CD-ROM (Danvers, MA: Pro CD)

The Ultimate Job Source CD-ROM (Orem, UT: InfoBusiness)

Win-Way Resume 3.0 CD-ROM (Sacramento, CA: Win-Way Corp.)

INDEX

189

CAREER RESOURCES

The following resources are available directly from Impact Publications. Complete this form or list the titles, include shipping (see the formula at the end), enclose payment, and send your order to:

IMPACT PUBLICATIONS
9104-N Manassas Drive
Manassas Park, VA 22111-5211
Tel. 703/361-7300, Fax 703/335-9486
E-mail: impactp@erols.com

Orders from individuals must be prepaid by check, moneyorder, Visa, MasterCard, or American Express number. We accept telephone and fax orders with a credit card number and signature. For updated information, visit Impact's World Wide Web site: http://www.impactpublications.com

Qty.	TITLES	Price	TOTAL
	NETWORKING		
___	Dynamite Networking for Dynamite Jobs	$15.95	___
___	Effective Networking	$9.95	___
___	Great Connections	$19.95	___
___	How to Use People and Get What You Want	$12.95	___
___	How to Work a Room	$9.95	___
___	Is Your "Net" Working?	$27.95	___
___	NBEW's Networking	$10.95	___
___	Network Your Way to Success	$19.95	___
___	Network Your Way to Your Next Job...Fast	$14.95	___
___	Power Networking	$14.95	___
___	Secrets of Savvy Networking	$10.95	___

ELECTRONIC NETWORKING

___ Be Your Own Headhunter Online	$16.00 ___
___ Electronic Job Search Revolution	$12.95 ___
___ Finding a Job on the Internet	$16.95 ___
___ Guide to Internet Job Searching	$14.95 ___
___ Hook Up, Get Hired	$12.95 ___
___ The Job-Seeker's Guide to On-Line Resources	$14.95 ___
___ Net Jobs: How to Use the Internet to Land Your Dream Job	$12.95 ___
___ On-Line Job Search Companion	$14.95 ___
___ Point and Click Jobfinder	$14.95 ___
___ Using the Internet in Your Job Search	$16.95 ___

JOB SEARCH STRATEGIES AND TACTICS

___ Adams Jobs Almanac 1996	$15.95 ___
___ Change Your Job, Change Your Life	$15.95 ___
___ Complete Idiot's Guide to Getting the Job You Want	$24.95 ___
___ Complete Job Finder's Guide to the 90's	$13.95 ___
___ Dynamite Tele-Search	$12.95 ___
___ Five Secrets to Finding a Job	$12.95 ___
___ How to Get Interviews From Classified Job Ads	$14.95 ___
___ How to Succeed Without a Career Path	$13.95 ___
___ Job Hunting for Dummies	$16.99 ___
___ Knock 'Em Dead 1996	$12.95 ___
___ Rites of Passage at $100,000+	$29.95 ___
___ What Color Is Your Parachute?	$14.95 ___

BEST JOBS AND EMPLOYERS FOR THE 90's

___ 100 Best Companies to Work for in America	$27.95 ___
___ 100 Best Jobs for the 1990s and Beyond	$19.95 ___
___ 101 Careers	$18.95 ___
___ 150 Companies for Liberal Arts Graduates	$12.95 ___
___ Adams Jobs Almanac 1996	$15.00 ___
___ American Almanac of Jobs and Salaries	$17.00 ___
___ Best Jobs for the 1990s and Into the 21st Century	$19.95 ___
___ Careers Encyclopedia	$39.95 ___
___ Hoover's Guide to Computer Companies (with disk)	$34.95 ___
___ Hoover's Masterlist of 2,500 of America's Largest and Fastest Growing Employers (with disk)	$19.95 ___
___ Job Seeker's Guide to 1000 Top Employers	$22.95 ___
___ Jobs 1996	$15.00 ___
___ Jobs Rated Almanac	$16.95 ___
___ Quantum Companies	$21.95 ___

RESUMES AND LETTERS

___ 175 High-Impact Cover Letters	$10.95 ___
___ 200 Letters for Job Hunters	$19.95 ___
___ Blue Collar and Beyond	$8.95 ___
___ Cover Letters That Knock 'Em Dead	$10.95 ___

___ Dynamite Cover Letters	$13.95	_____
___ Dynamite Resumes	$13.95	_____
___ Electronic Resume Revolution	$12.95	_____
___ Electronic Resumes	$19.95	_____
___ Electronic Resumes for the New Job Market	$11.95	_____
___ Gallery of Best Resumes	$16.95	_____
___ High Impact Resumes and Letters	$14.95	_____
___ Job Search Letters That Get Results	$15.95	_____
___ Ready-to-Go Resumes	$29.95	_____
___ Resume Catalog	$15.95	_____
___ Resume Pro	$24.95	_____
___ Resumes That Knock 'Em Dead	$10.95	_____

INTERVIEWS & SALARY NEGOTIATIONS

___ 60 Seconds and You're Hired!	$ 9.95	_____
___ 101 Dynamite Questions to Ask At Your Job Interview	$14.95	_____
___ 101 Dynamite Ways to Ace the Job Interview	$13.95	_____
___ 101 Great Answers to the Toughest Interview Questions	$9.95	_____
___ Conquer Interview Objections	$10.95	_____
___ Dynamite Answers to Interview Questions	$11.95	_____
___ Dynamite Salary Negotiation	$13.95	_____
___ Interview for Success	$15.95	_____
___ Interview Power	$12.95	_____
___ Naked At the Interview	$10.95	_____
___ Perfect Interview	$17.95	_____
___ Power Interviews	$12.95	_____
___ Sweaty Palms	$8.95	_____

DRESS, APPEARANCE, IMAGE

___ 110 Mistakes Working Women Make/Dressing Smart	$9.95	_____
___ John Molloy's New Dress for Success	$10.95	_____
___ Red Socks Don't Work! (Men's Clothing)	$14.95	_____

KEY DIRECTORIES

___ American Salaries and Wages Survey	$115.00	_____
___ Dictionary of Occupational Titles	$39.95	_____
___ Directory of Executive Recruiters	$44.95	_____
___ Encyclopedia of Associations	$1,149.00	_____
___ Encyclopedia of Careers & Vocational Guidance	$129.95	_____
___ Hoover's Handbook of American Companies	$29.95	_____
___ Hoover's Handbook of World Business	$27.95	_____
___ Internships 1996	$21.95	_____
___ Job Bank Guide to Employment Services	$159.95	_____
___ Job Hunter's Sourcebook	$69.95	_____
___ Moving and Relocation Directory	$179.95	_____
___ National Job Bank	$269.95	_____
___ National Trade and Professional Associations	$79.95	_____
___ Occupational Outlook Handbook	$21.95	_____
___ Personnel Executives Contactbook	$149.00	_____

__ Professional Careers Sourcebook $89.95 _____
__ Vocational Careers Sourcebook $79.95 _____

TELEPHONE AND JOB HOTLINE DIRECTORIES

__ Government Directory of Addresses
    and Telephone Numbers $165.00 _____
__ Job Hotlines USA $24.95 _____
__ Job Hunter's Yellow Pages $35.00 _____
__ National Directory of Addresses and
    Telephone Numbers $125.00 _____

JOB VACANCY SOURCEBOOKS

__ Government Job Finder $16.95 _____
·_ Non-Profits' Job Finder $16.95 _____
__ Professional's Private Sector Job Finder $18.95 _____

CITY AND STATE JOB FINDERS (Adams Media's JobBanks)

__ Atlanta $15.95 _____
__ Boston $15.95 _____
__ Chicago $15.95 _____
__ Dallas/Fort Worth $15.95 _____
__ Denver $15.95 _____
__ Florida $15.95 _____
__ Houston $15.95 _____
__ Los Angeles $15.95 _____
__ Minneapolis $15.95 _____
__ New York $15.95 _____
__ Philadelphia $15.95 _____
__ San Francisco $15.95 _____
__ Seattle $15.95 _____
__ Washington, DC $15.95 _____

CITY AND STATE JOB FINDERS (Surrey Books)

__ Atlanta $15.95 _____
__ Boston $15.95 _____
__ Dallas/Fort Worth $15.95 _____
__ Houston $15.95 _____
__ New York $15.95 _____
__ San Francisco $15.95 _____
__ Seattle and Portland $15.95 _____
__ Southern California $15.95 _____
__ Washington, DC $15.95 _____

INTERNATIONAL, OVERSEAS, AND TRAVEL JOBS

__ Almanac of International Jobs and Careers $19.95 _____
__ Complete Guide to International Jobs & Careers $13.95 _____
__ Guide to Careers in World Affairs $14.95 _____

___ How to Get a Job in Europe $17.95 _____
___ How to Get a Job in the Pacific Rim $17.95 _____
___ Jobs for People Who Love Travel $15.95 _____
___ Jobs in Russia and the Newly Independent States $15.95 _____
___ Jobs Worldwide $17.95 _____

GOVERNMENT AND NONPROFIT CAREERS

___ Complete Guide to Public Employment $19.95 _____
___ Directory of Federal Jobs and Employers $21.95 _____
___ Federal Applications That Get Results $23.95 _____
___ Federal Jobs in Law Enforcement $14.95 _____
___ Federal Jobs in Nursing and Health Sciences $14.95 _____
___ Find a Federal Job Fast! $13.95 _____
___ Government Job Finder $16.95 _____
___ Jobs and Careers With Nonprofit Organizations $15.95 _____

SKILLS, TESTING, SELF-ASSESSMENT

___ Discover the Best Jobs for You $11.95 _____
___ Do What You Are $16.95 _____
___ Do What You Love, the Money Will Follow $11.95 _____
___ I Could Do Anything If I Only Knew What It Was $19.95 _____
___ Wishcraft $11.95 _____

MILITARY

___ From Air Force Blue to Corporate Gray $17.95 _____
___ From Army Green to Corporate Gray $15.95 _____
___ From Navy Blue to Corporate Gray $17.95 _____

MINORITIES AND DISABLED

___ Best Companies for Minorities $12.00 _____
___ Big Book of Minority Opportunities $39.95 _____
___ Job Strategies for People With Disabilities $14.95 _____
___ Minority Organizations $49.95 _____

ENTREPRENEURSHIP AND SELF-EMPLOYMENT

___ 101 Best Businesses to Start $15.00 _____
___ Best Home-Based Businesses for the 90s $12.95 _____
___ Entrepreneur's Guide to Starting a Successful Business $16.95 _____

COMPUTER SOFTWARE PROGRAMS (IBM or Compatibles)

___ Cambridge Career Counseling System $349.00 _____
___ INSTANT™ Job Hunting Letters $39.95 _____
___ JOBHUNT™ for Window® $59.95 _____
___ Resumemaker™ With Career Planning $49.95 _____
___ You're Hired! $59.95 _____

CD-ROM

__ Electronic Guide for Occupational Exploration	$295.00	_____
__ Encyclopedia of Careers and Vocational Guidance	$199.95	_____
__ Multimedia Career Center	$385.00	_____
__ Resume Revolution	$99.00	_____
__ Ultimate Job Source (Individual Version)	$49.95	_____
__ Ultimate Job Source (Professional Version)	$199.95	_____
__ Win-Way Resume 3.0	$69.95	_____

SUBTOTAL   _____

Virginia residents add 4½% sales tax   _____

POSTAGE/HANDLING ($4 for first
product and $1 for each additional) $4.00

Number of additional titles x $1.00 ---------- _____

Add 5% of retail for $49.95+ items------------ _____

TOTAL ENCLOSED ----------------- _____

NAME _____

ADDRESS _____

_____

_____

❏ I enclose check/moneyorder for $ _____ made payable to
IMPACT PUBLICATIONS.

❏ Please charge $ _____ to my credit card:
   ❏ Visa   ❏ MasterCard   ❏ American Express

Card # _____

Expiration date: _____/_____

Signature _____

SEND TO: **IMPACT PUBLICATIONS**, 9104-N Manassas Drive,
Manassas Park, VA 22111-5211, Tel. 703/361-7300 or
Fax 703/335-9486